I0391215

A coloring book by **Brian K Boeck** aka **Photos by Brick**
Current location: Bangkok Thailand
www.photosbybrick.com
www.instagram.com/bkbnbkk

Stories, Photos and Design by Brian K Boeck
Illustration by Madison White

A Coloring Rooftop Tour: Bangkok

Prepare for your coloring journey across Bangkok city with unique heights and urban landscape.

A coloring book of real Bangkok locations

All pictures are from actual photography from hard to reach locations. Enjoy the rooftop tour!

Sometimes looking up with a purpose creates a lasting memory, especially if you have your camera at the ready. Taken near Sala Daeng BTS, Bangkok

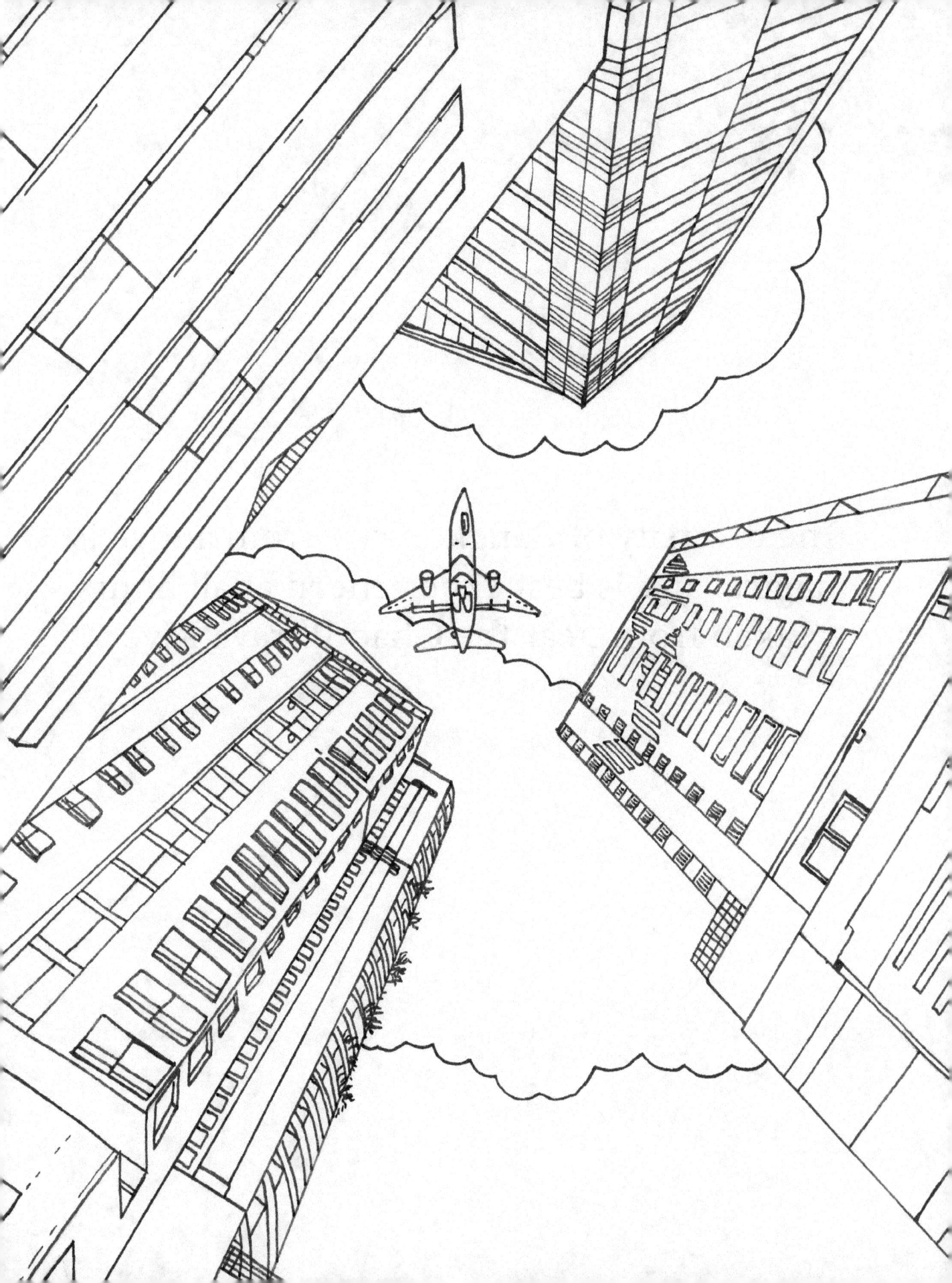

The diversity of Bangkok city from above is magical and is best experienced at all hours. Taken from near the Chao Phraya River.

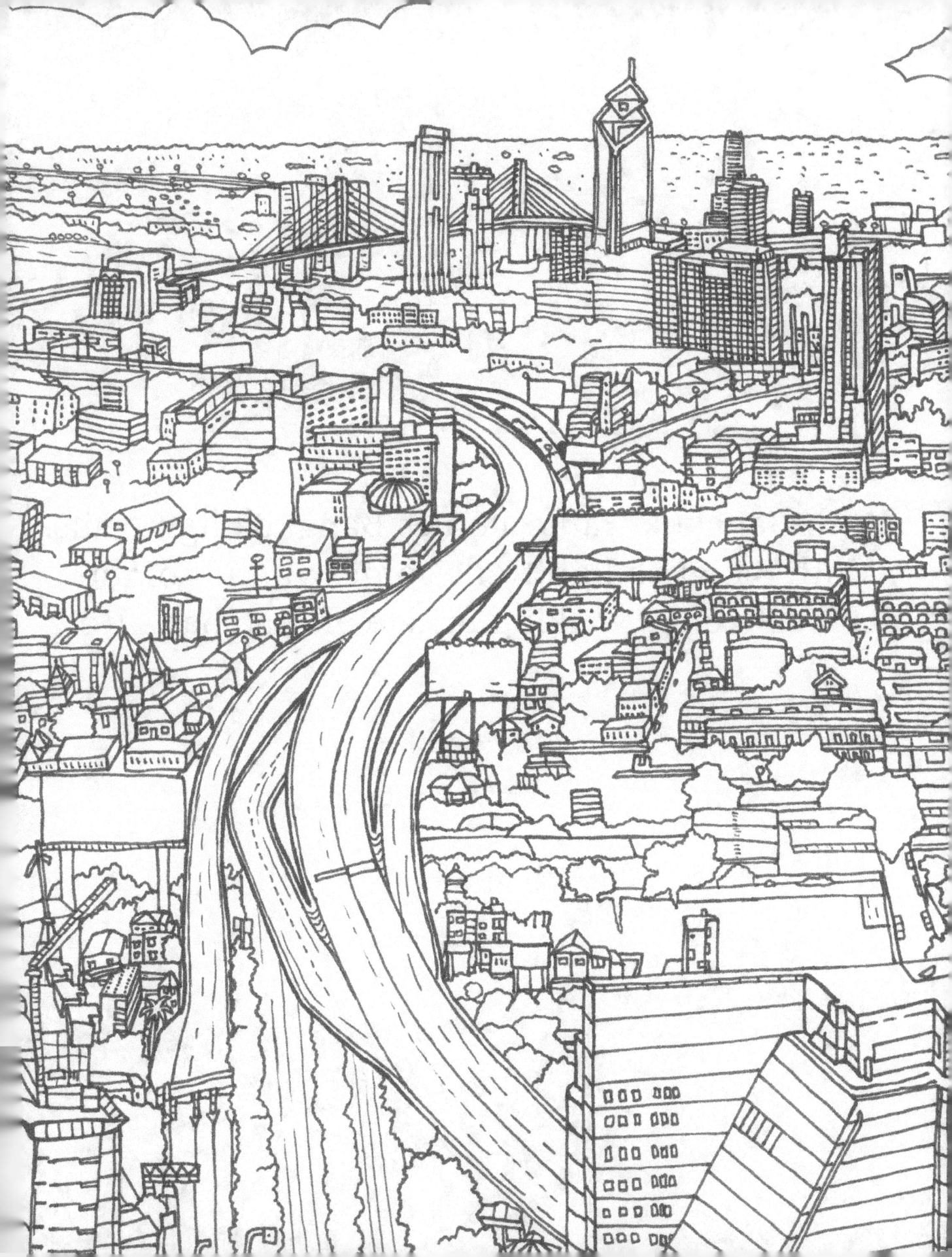

With Bangkok traffic, comes Bangkok lighttrails. With Bangkok lighttrails comes vibrant nights. Taken from a walking bridge on Ratchada Rd.

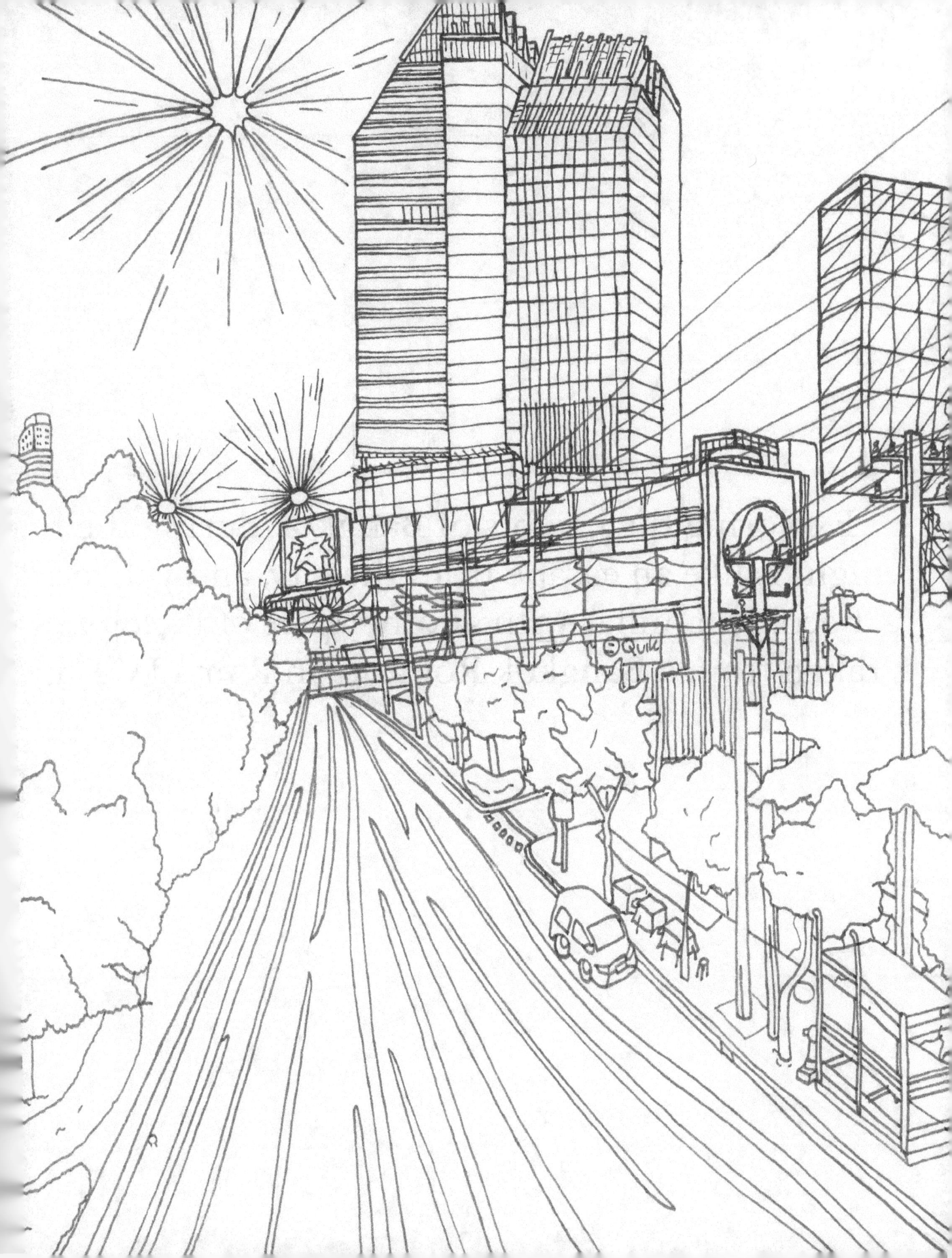

Exploring the heights of Bangkok during the night is like an escape from the city, and yet you become familiar with another part of the city. Taken from a Bangkok Rooftop on Rama IV Rd.

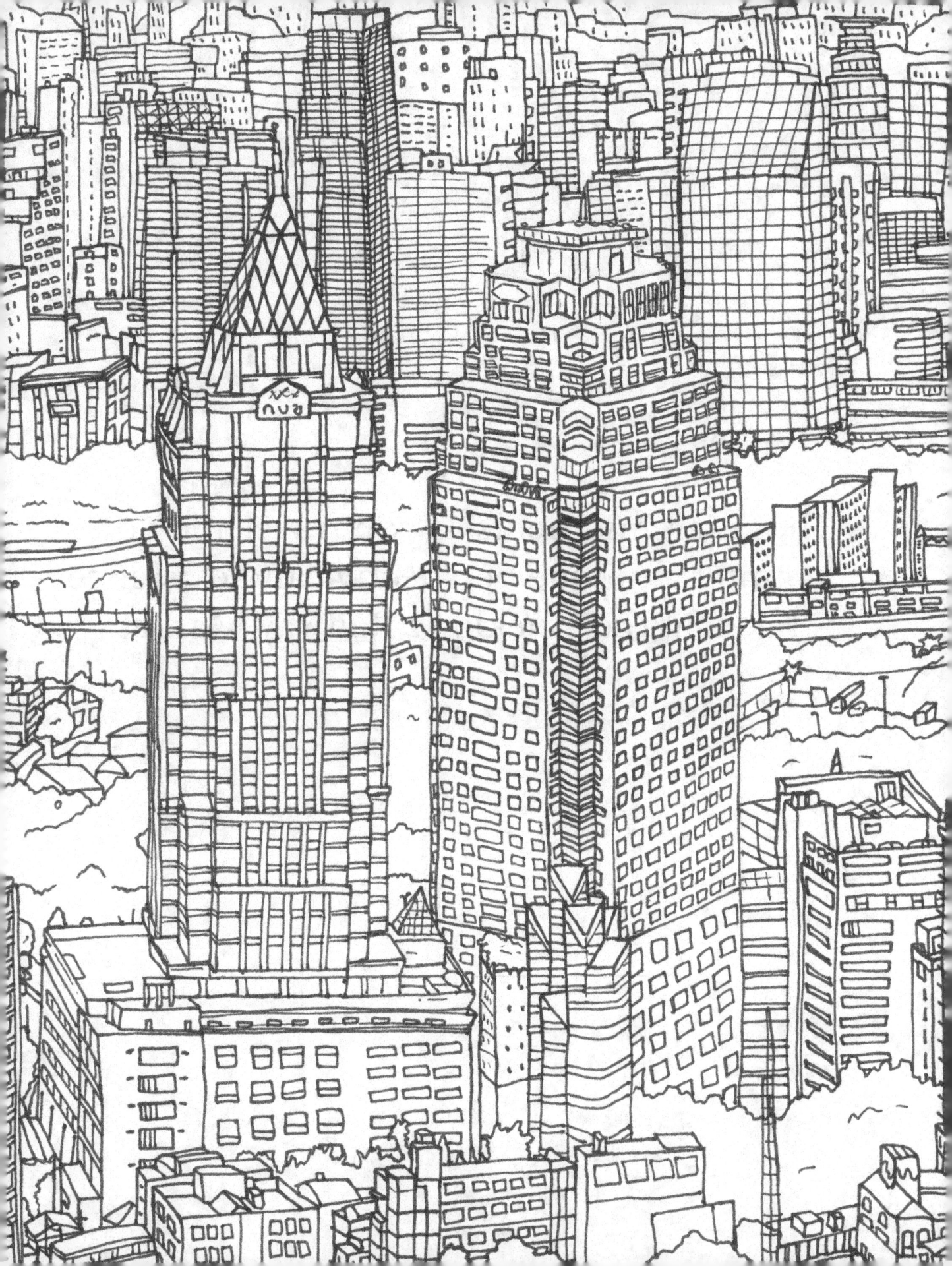

Those rare moments as you travel and you encounter a unique perspective and existence. Taken at the Maeklong Railway Market

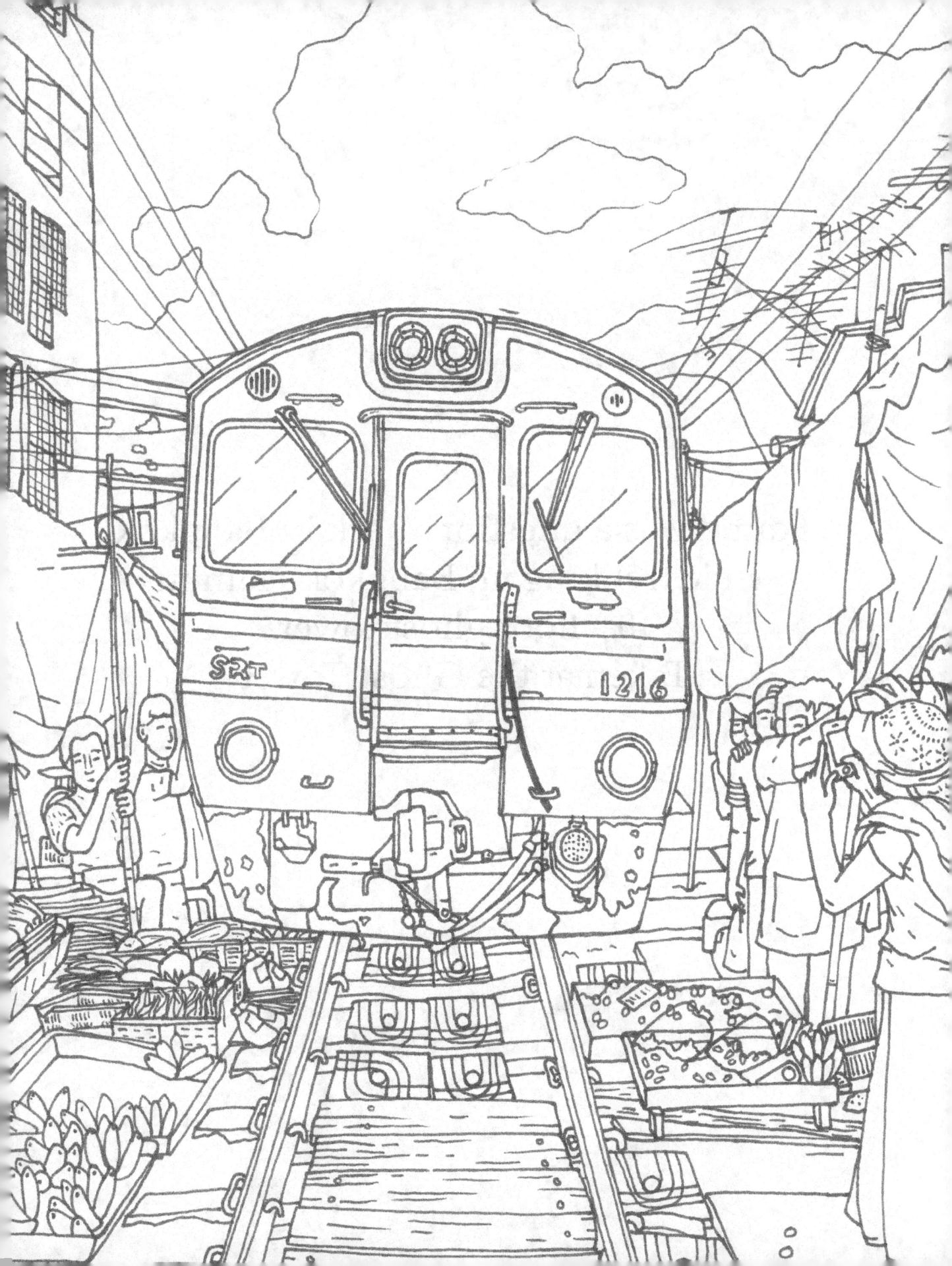

Found was a question mark in Bangkok
while trekking up Bangkok's famous
40+ floor ghost tower.
Taken at the Ghost Tower

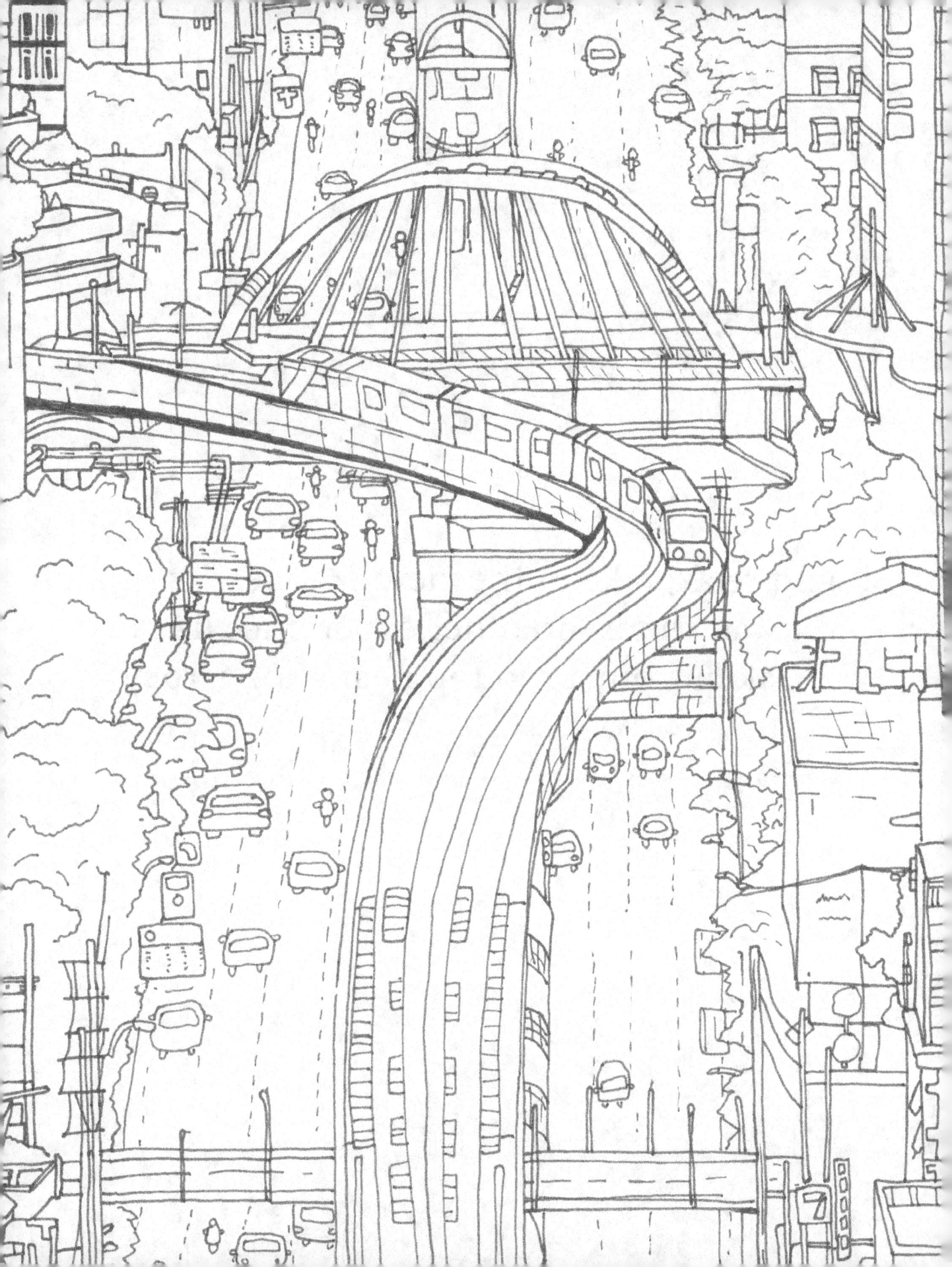

Sit and relax, take in the view. Dangerous though it was, theres no other experience like it. Taken from a rooftop near Klong Toey

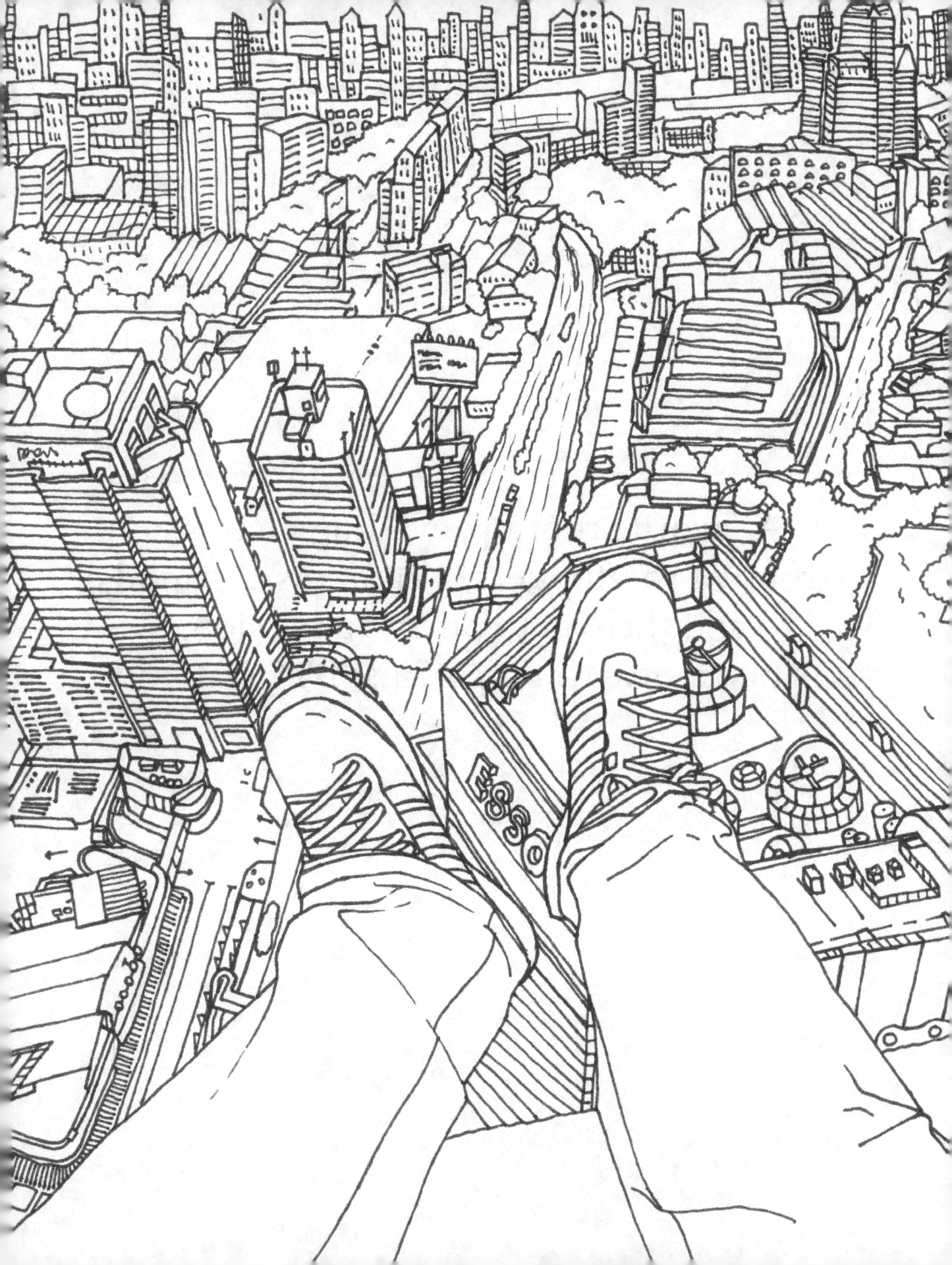

A favorite rooftop, evading guards, a group of rooftoppers, 3 cameras, 3 tripods, and the will to pursue a passion.
Taken near Chong Nonsi BTS station

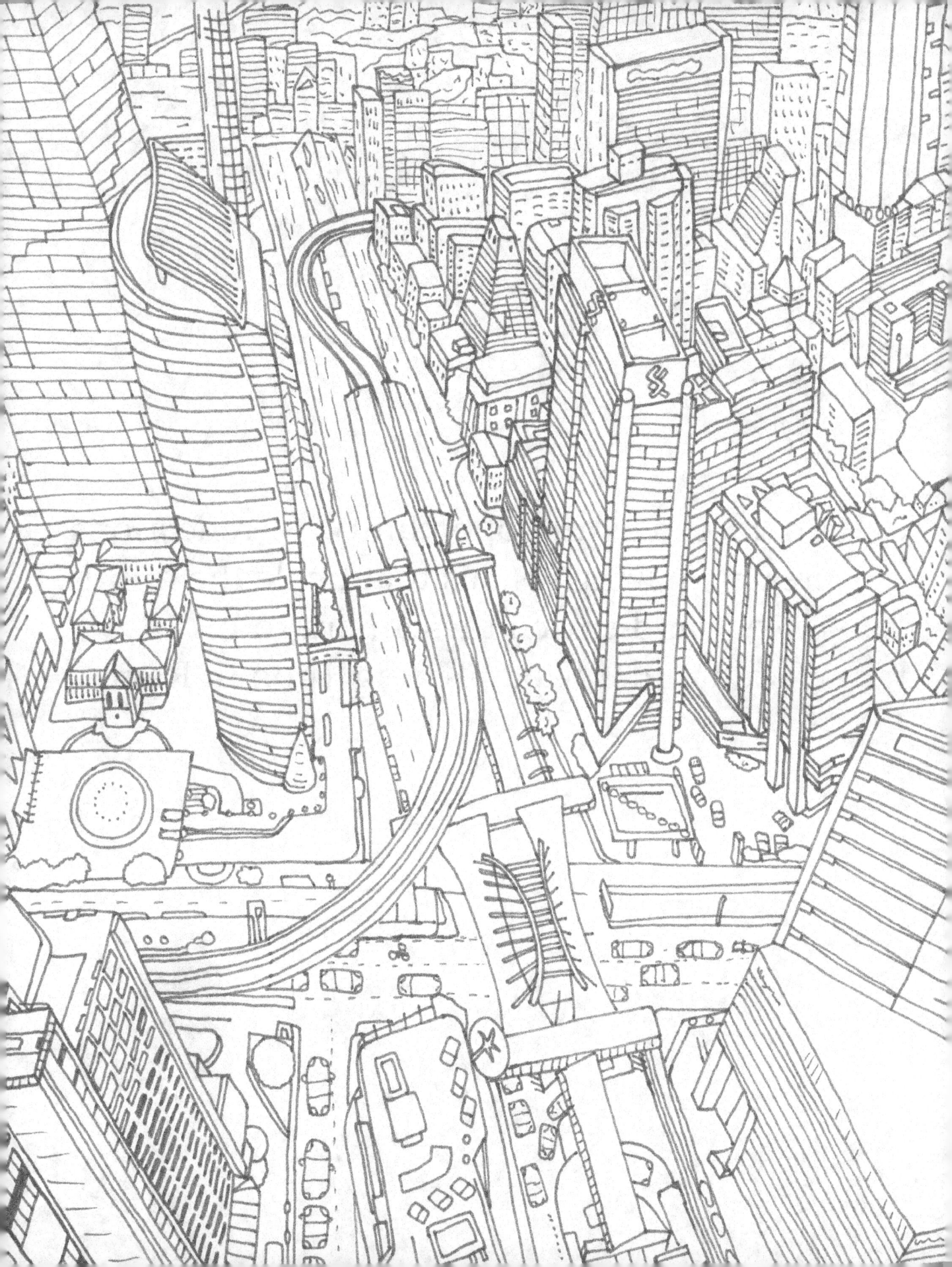

Rain, if seen as an opportunity for reflections, create amazing visuals that tickle the mind and enrich the camera roll.
Taken under Sapan Krung Thon in Rain

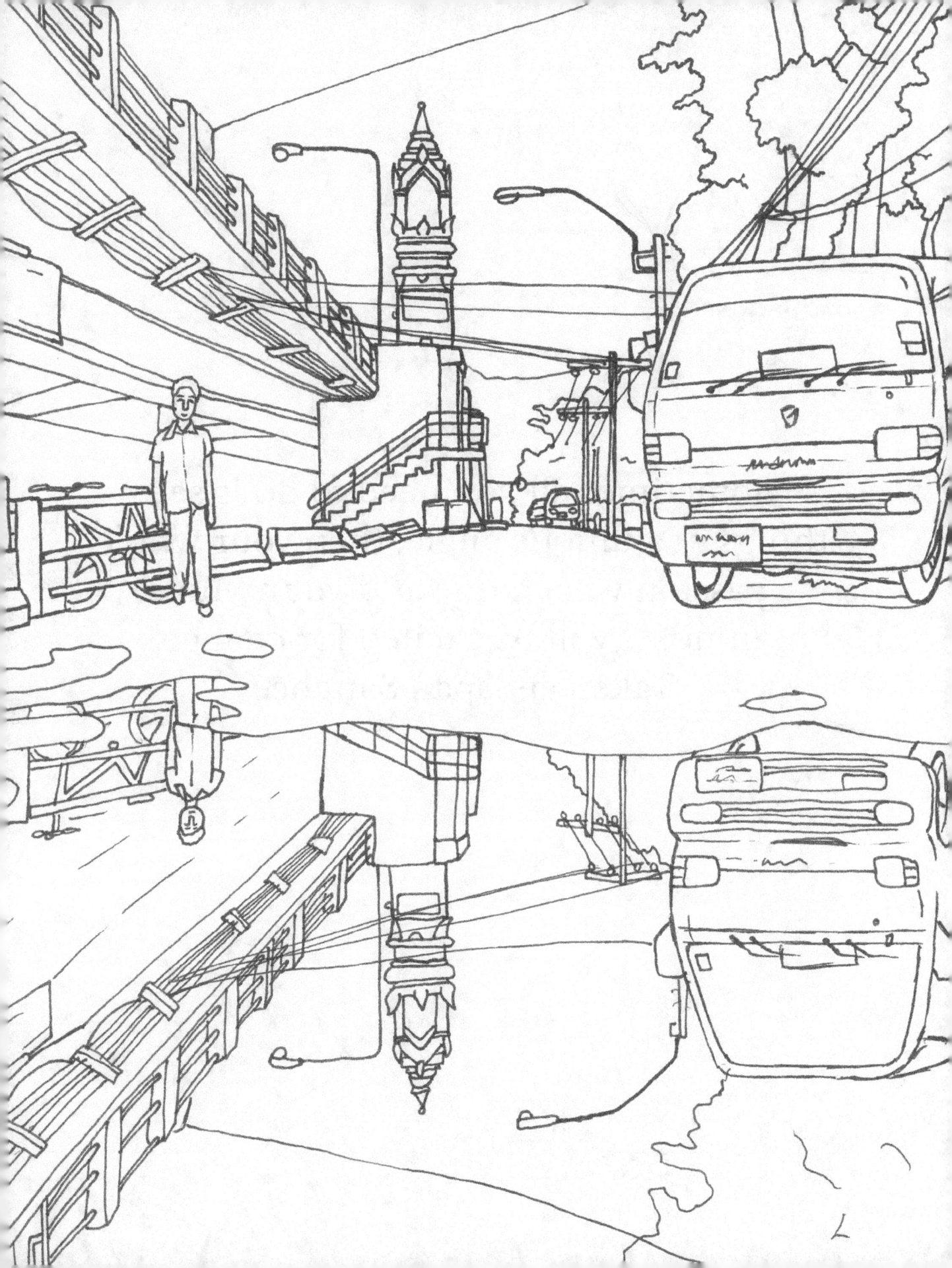

Sometimes all you need to do is see things in a unique angle, then your whole passion will charge and your whole mindset will be excited for change.
Taken at Sapan Sanghee

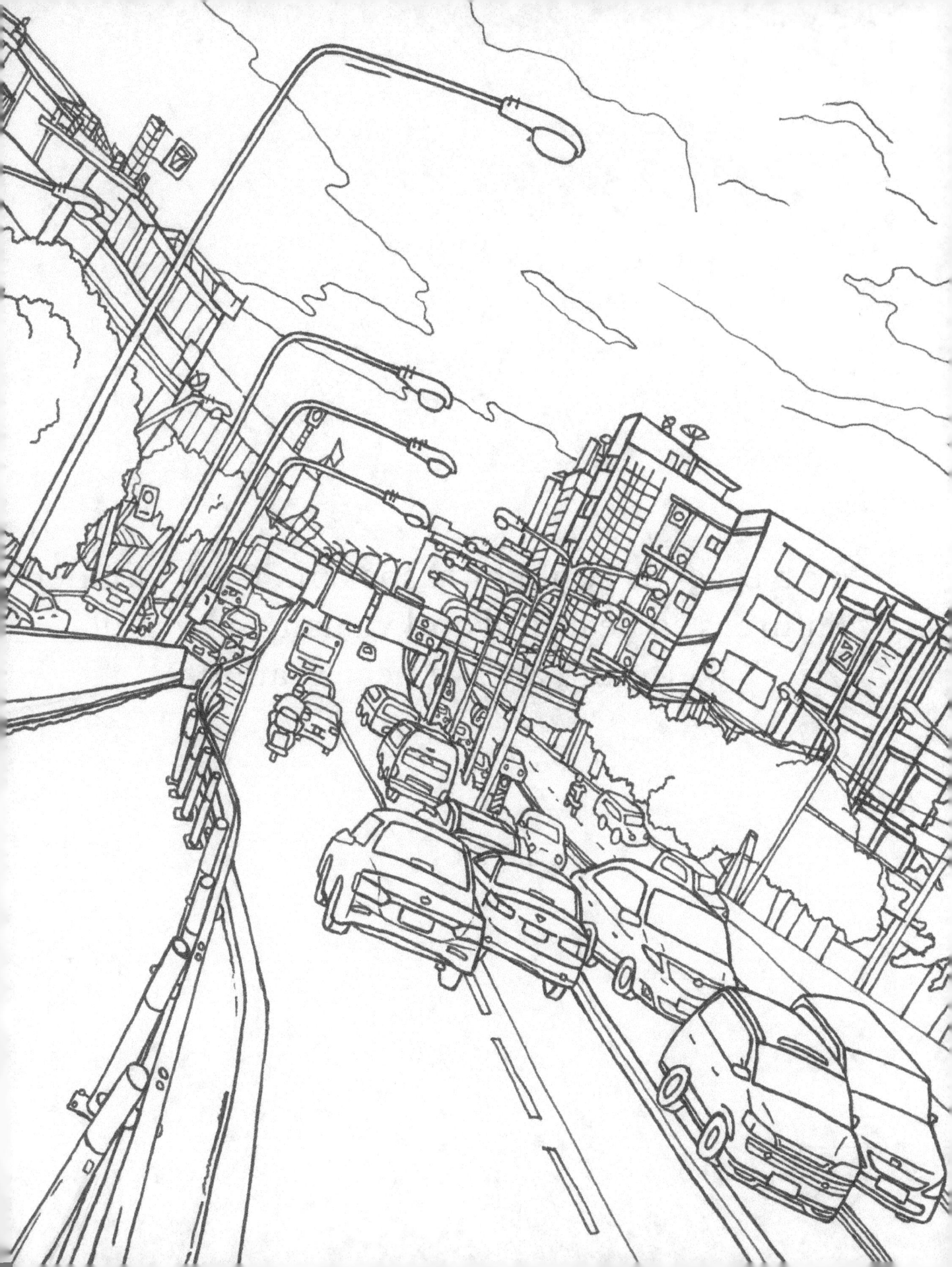

In a cave, as the sunlight rushes in. Its no wonder nature is so beautiful and visually powerful. Taken from a Cave near Pranburi

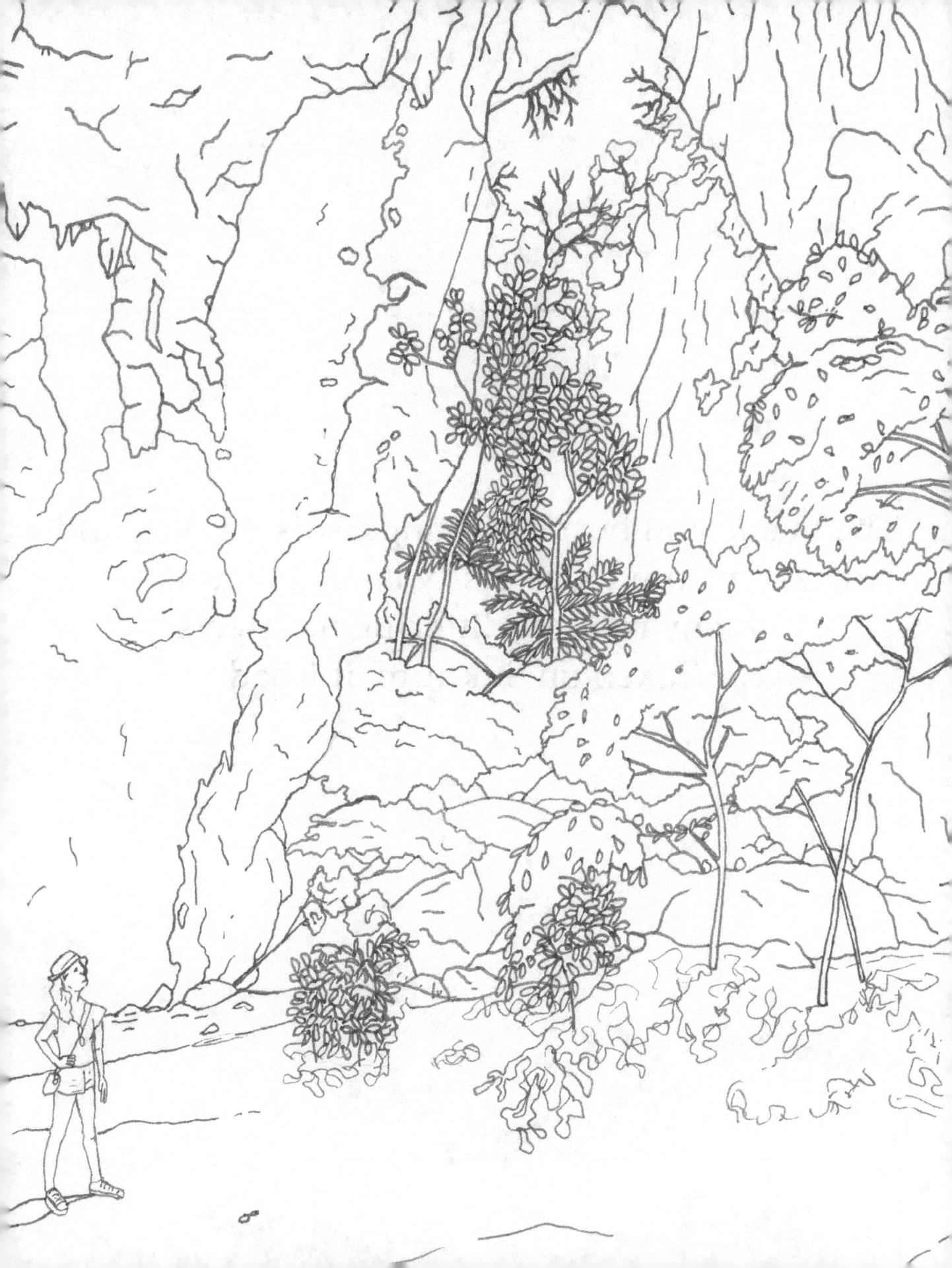

The hustle and bustle of Bangkok is unique, and a small rest from its diversity is easily found on the many rooftops littering its streets.
Taken on Sukhumvit Road

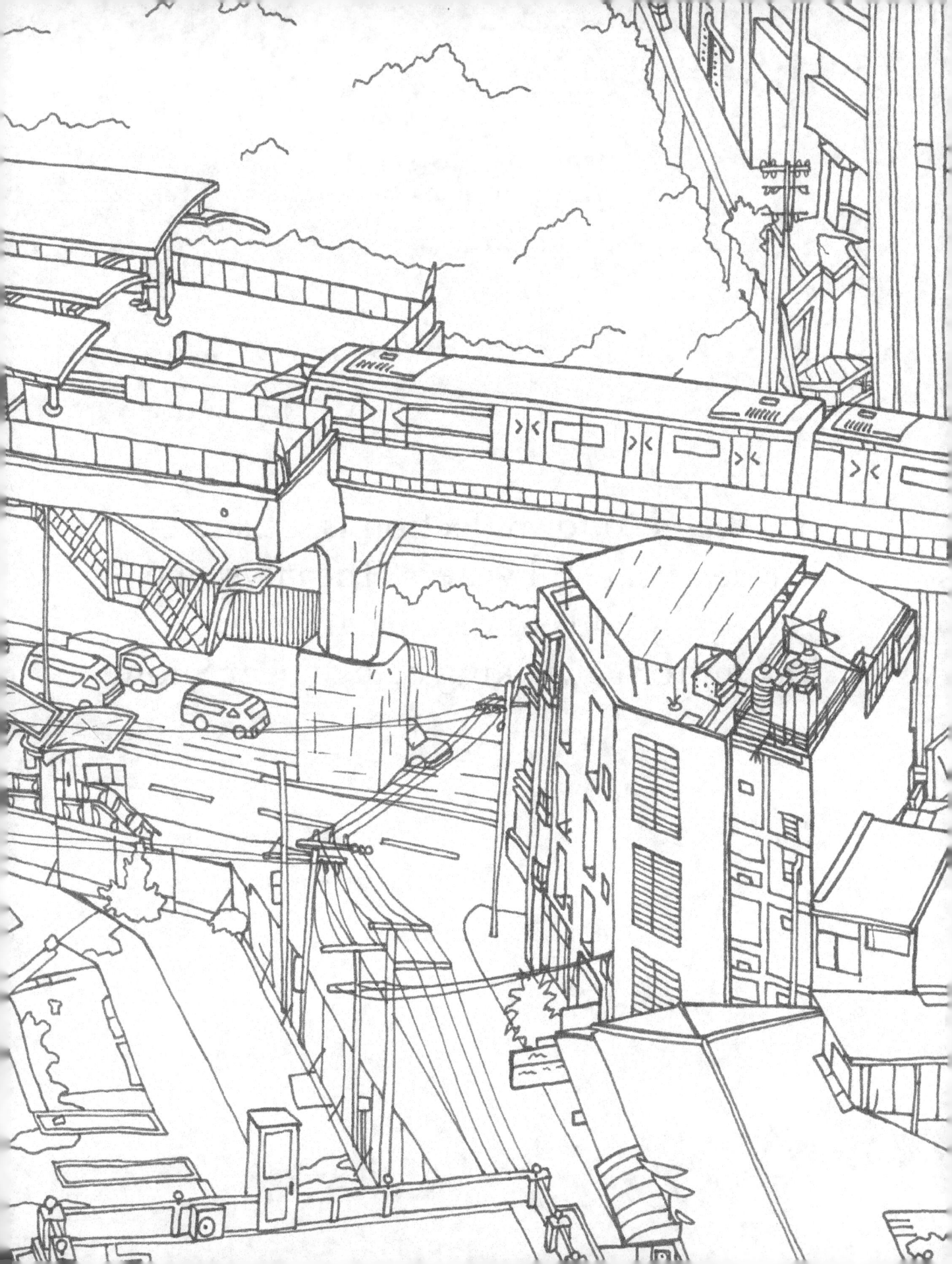

The need for reflection is satisfied
when near still waters. The cityscape
only adds to the visual verve.
Taken from a walking bridge near Silom

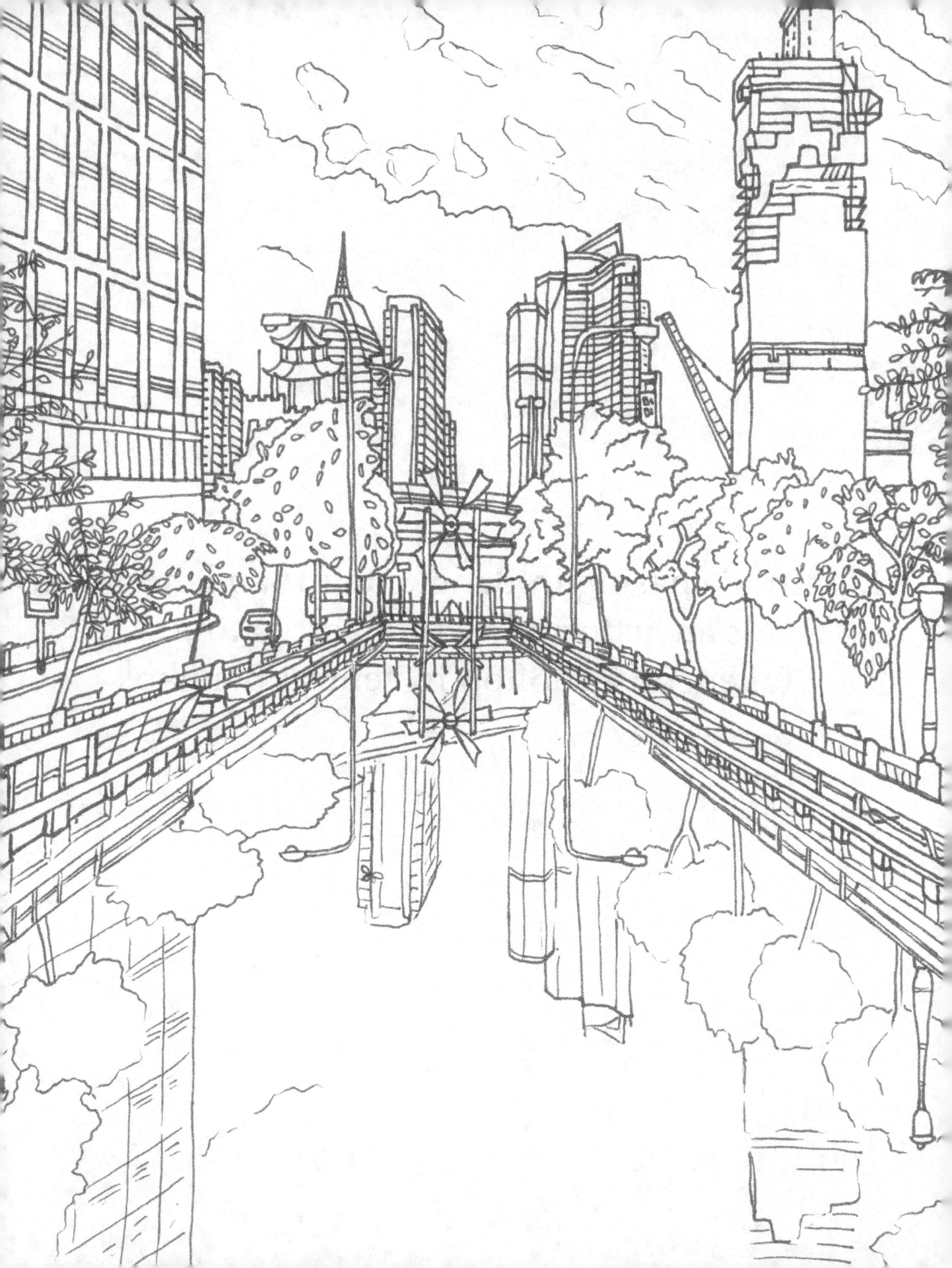

Lighttrail chasing in Bangkok's urban landscape,
is an artform worth investigating.
Taken on a rooftop in central Bangkok

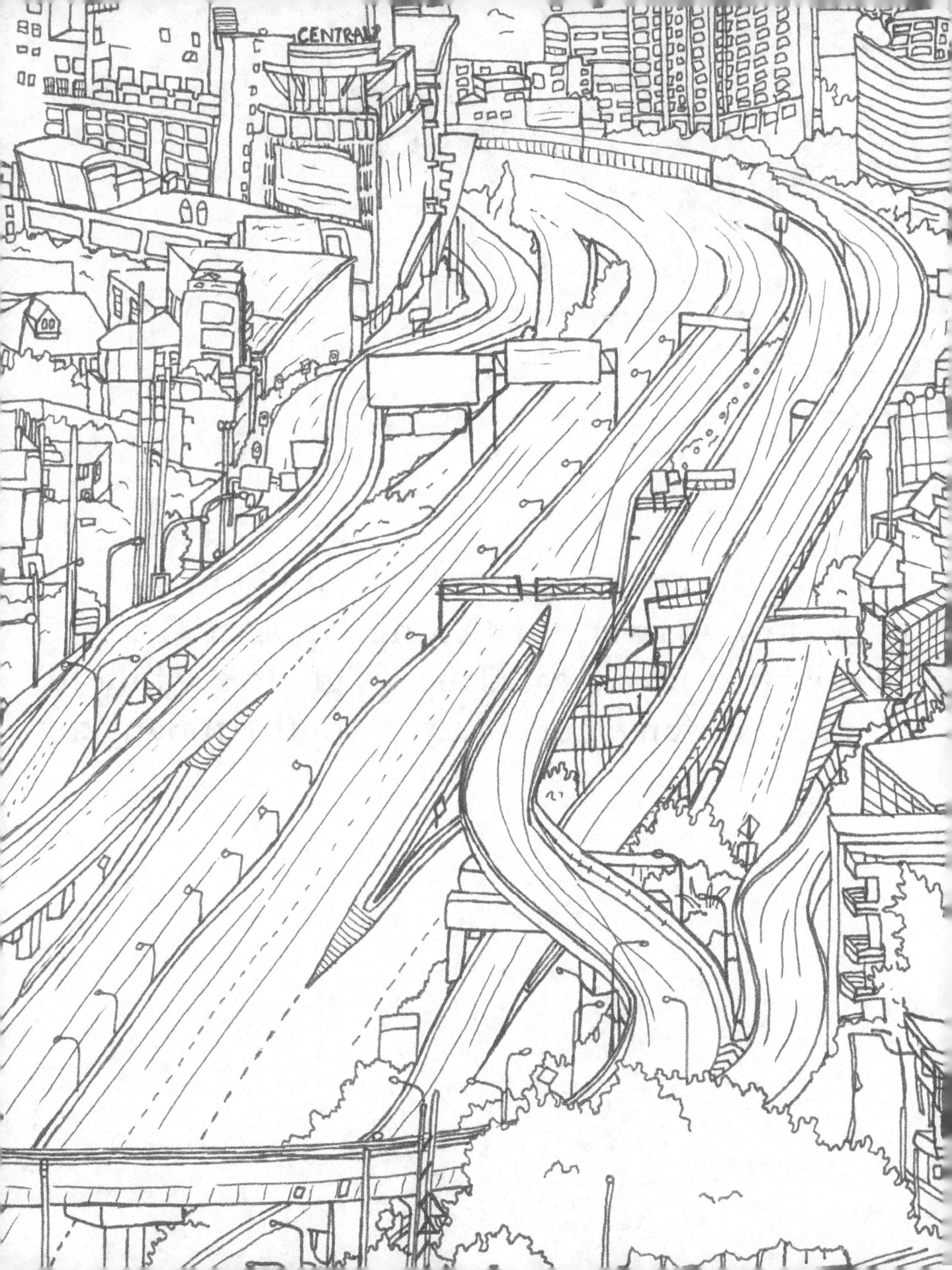

The only way to reflect a night in a flowing river is with long exposure. The visual treasures created are a sight to see indeed. Taken near an express way in southern Bangkok

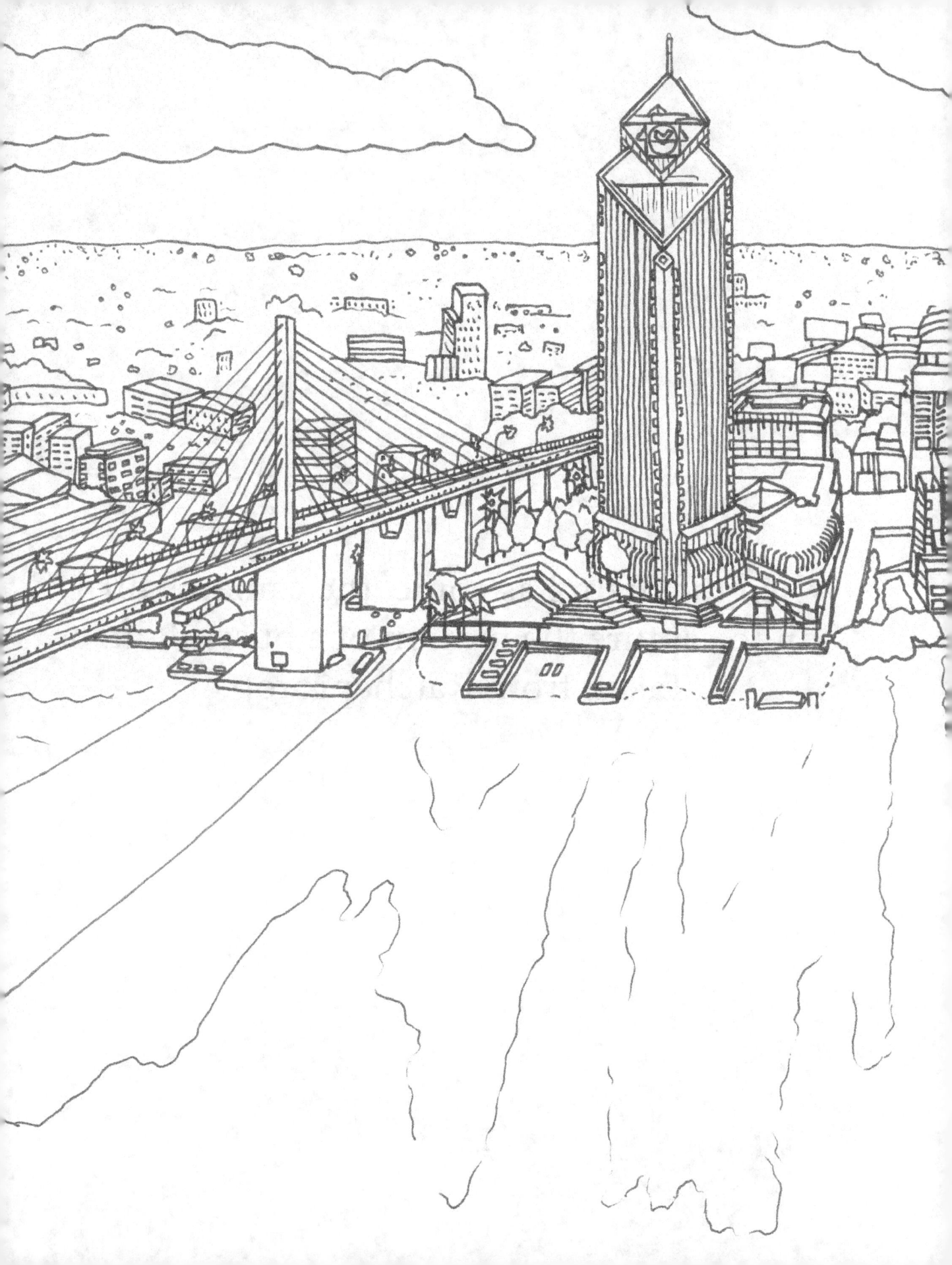

When the night has come, the cameras turn on to capture the motion of a busy night.
Taken from Ratchaprorop

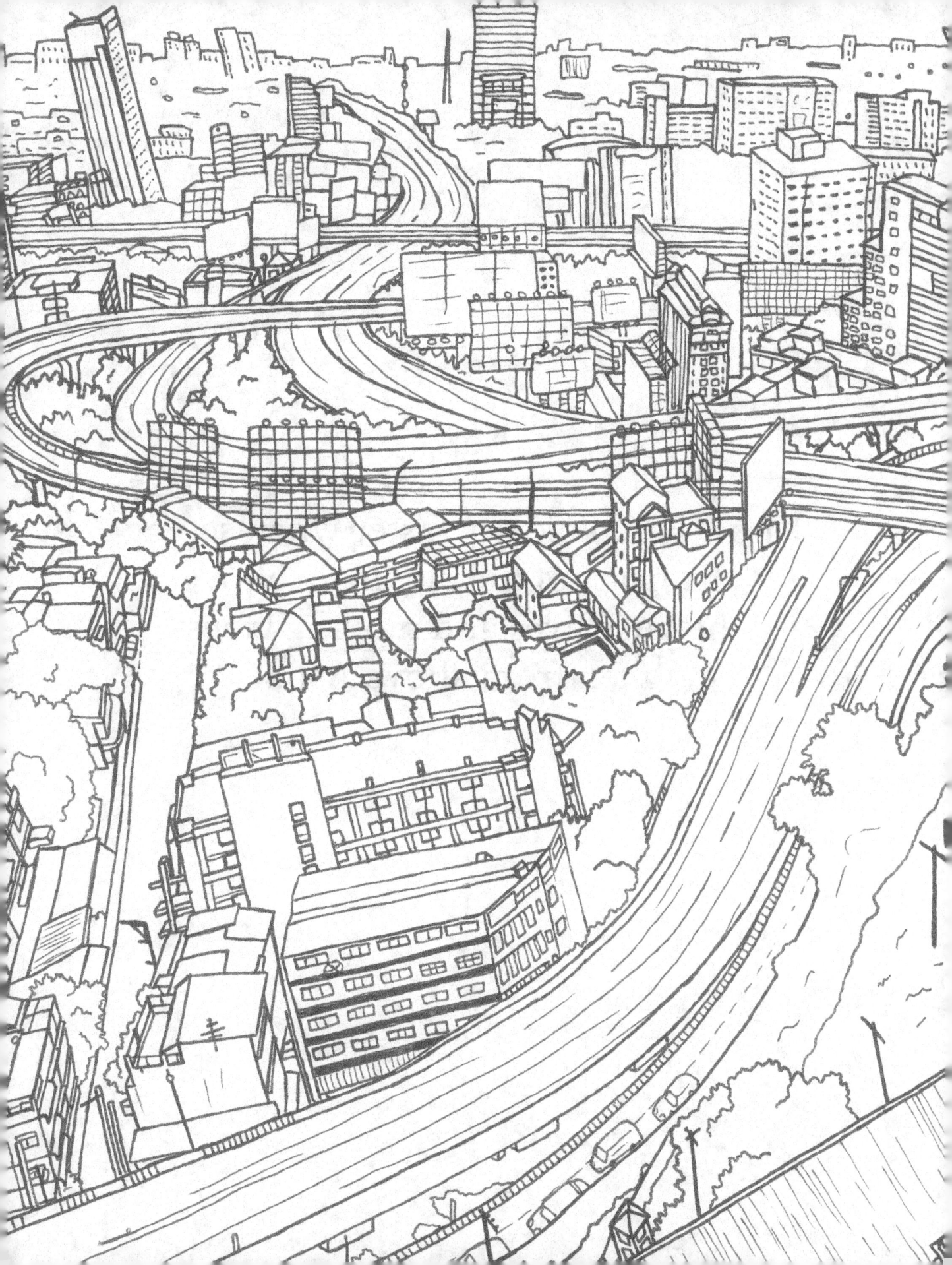

Know Bangkok city faster when seeing
the heart of the city from above
the busy lives and moving vibes.
Taken from above Asoke

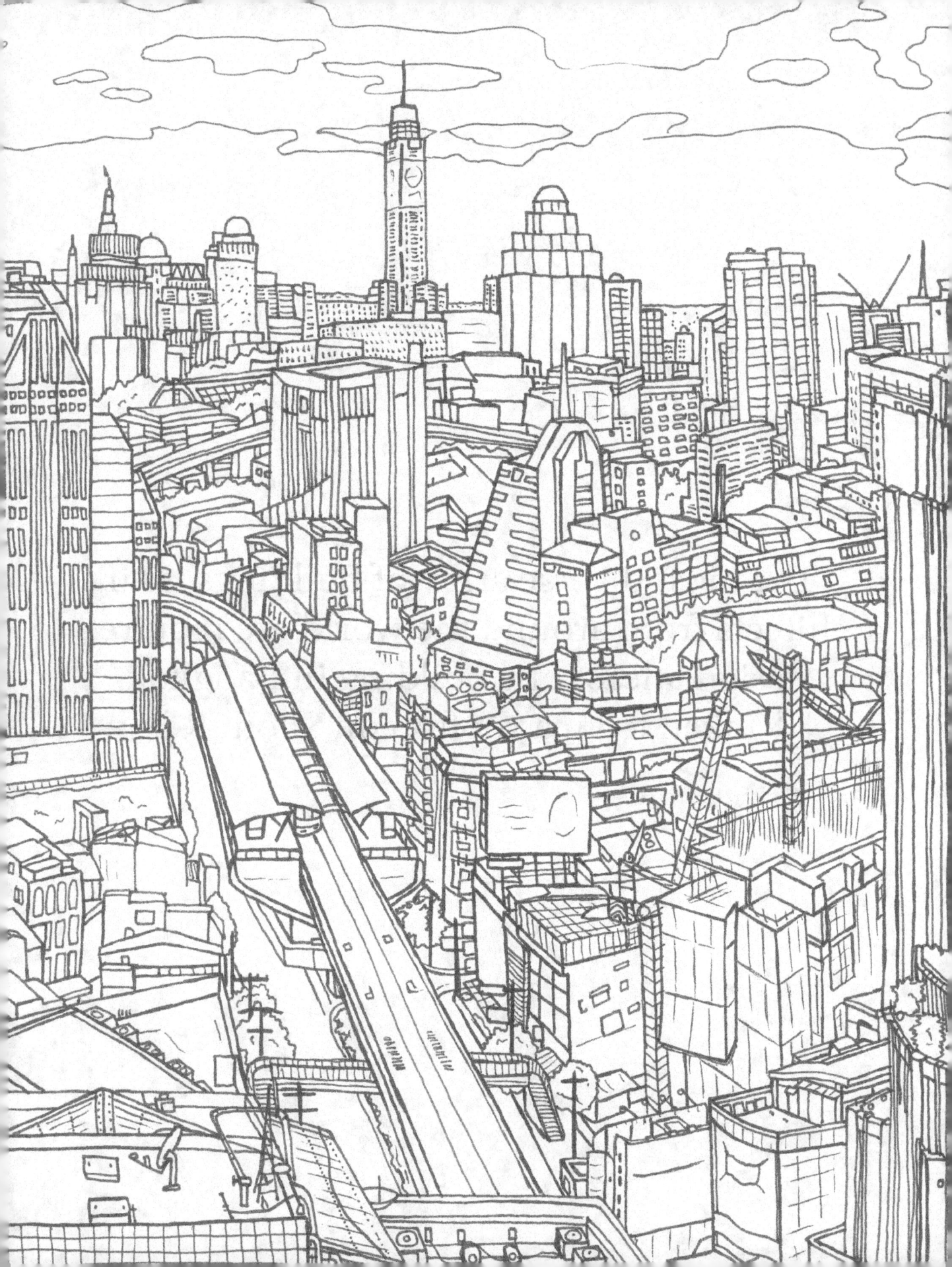

The most diverse array of buildings, as if architects from around the world are required to design atleast one building in Bangkok. Taken from a rooftop on Silom Rd

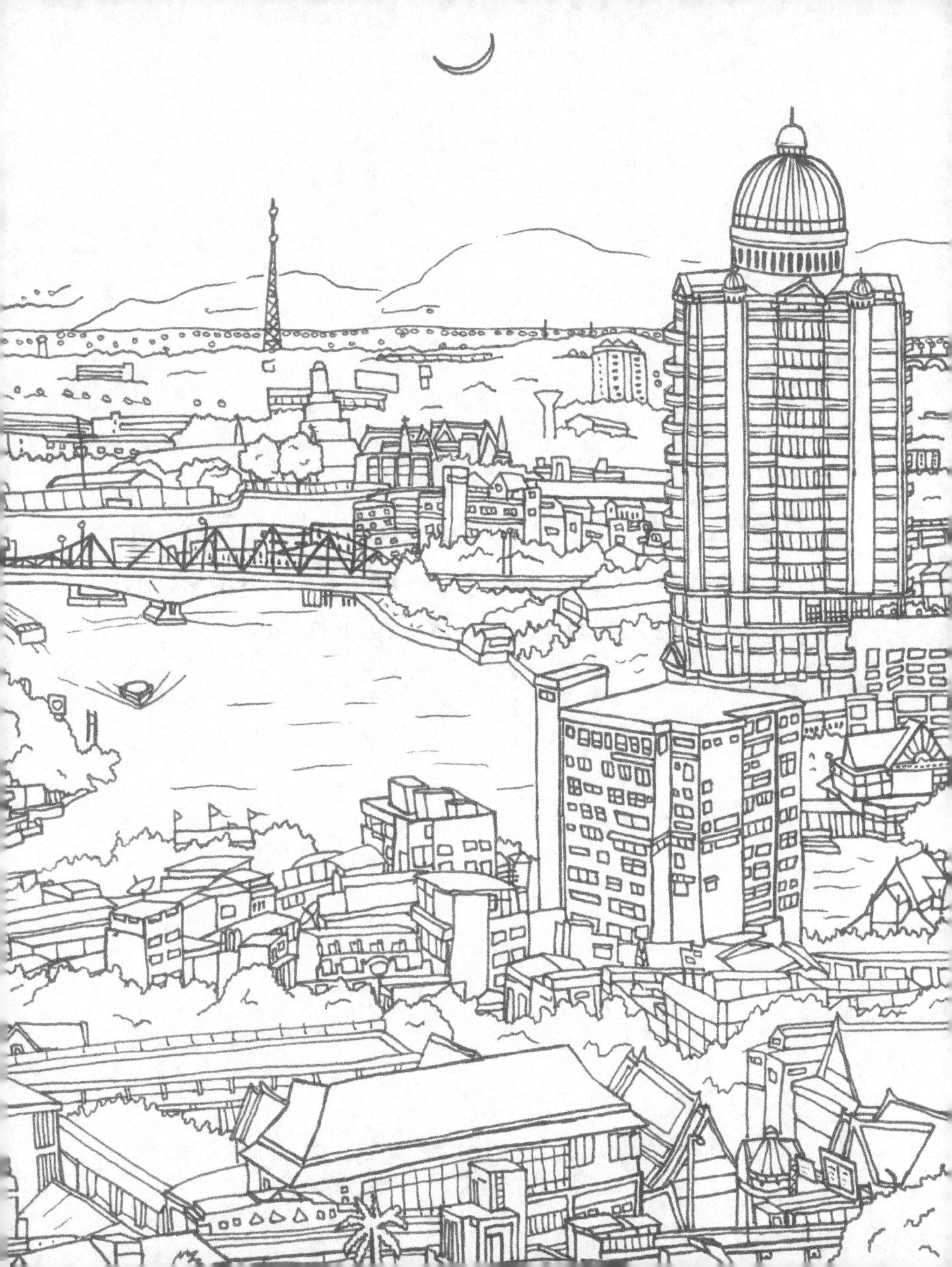

When up high, on a rooftop, the cityscape is not the only thing you can focus on.
Taken from Bang Phlat

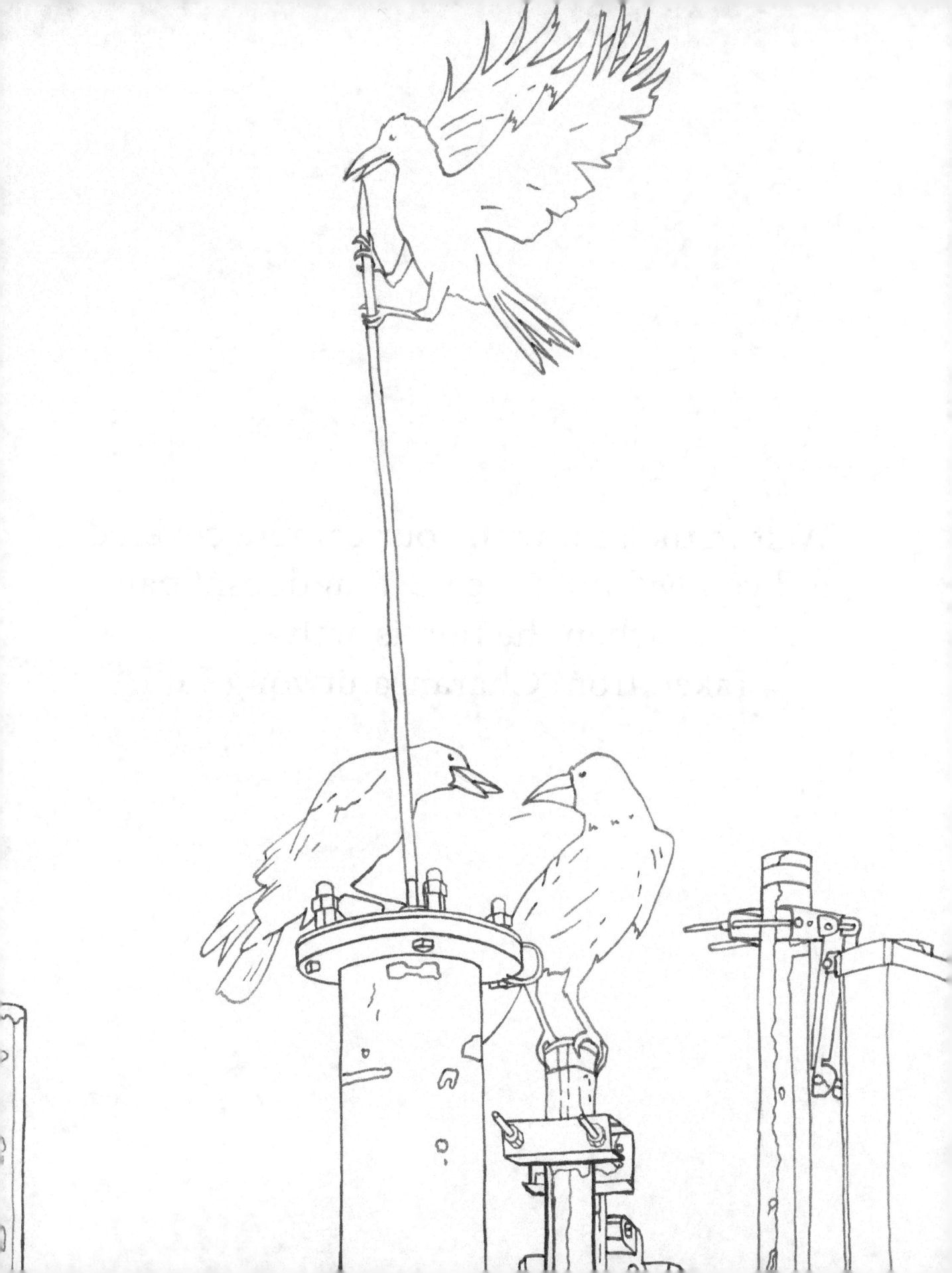

Wait in the rain with your camera covered and you will miss the life that doesnt pause when the rain is active.
Taken from Charansanitwong Rd

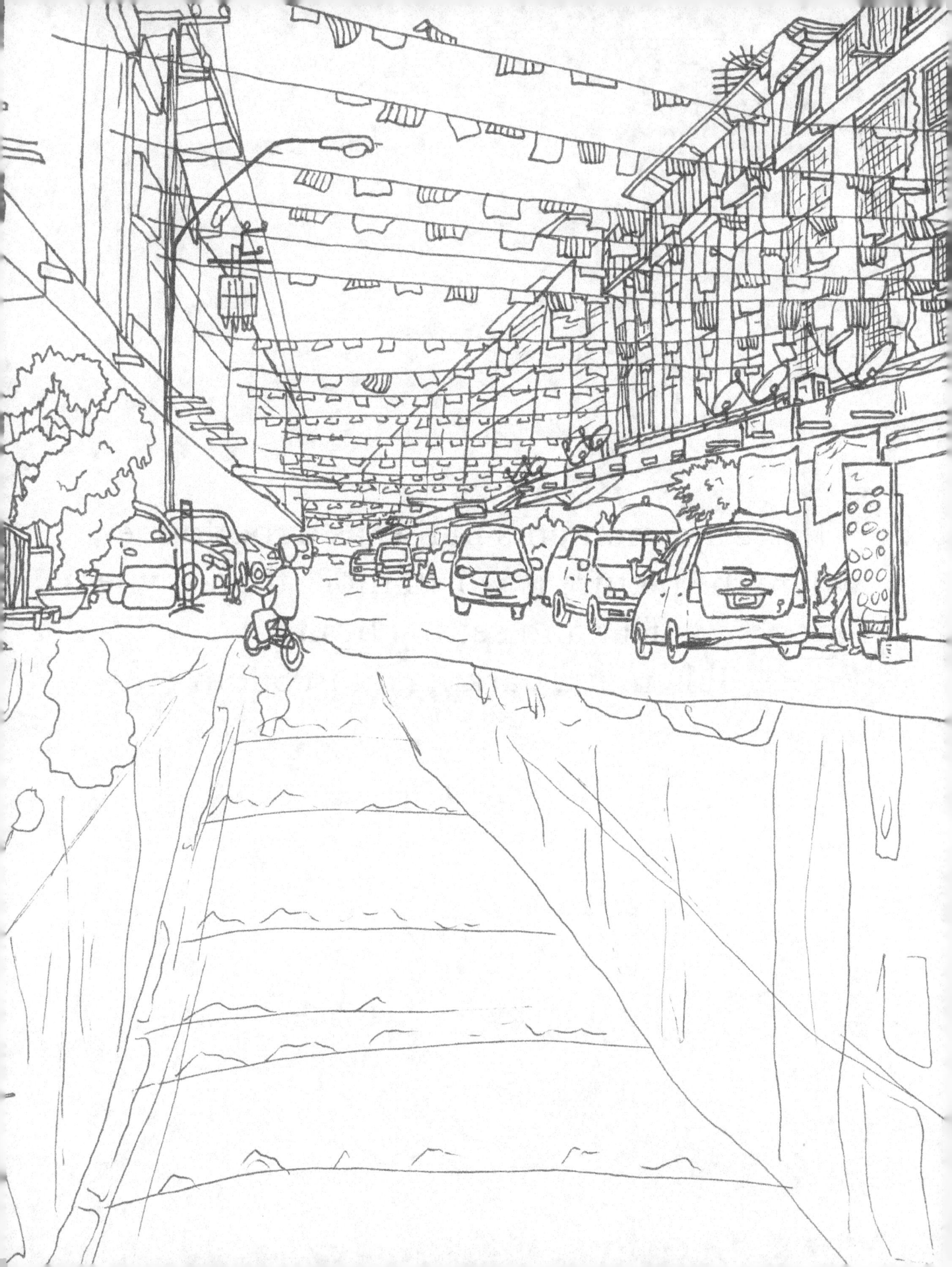

There are moments in life, as a rooftopper, where the picture is worth more than shyness, fear and setting limits.
Taken in a parking lot in Silom

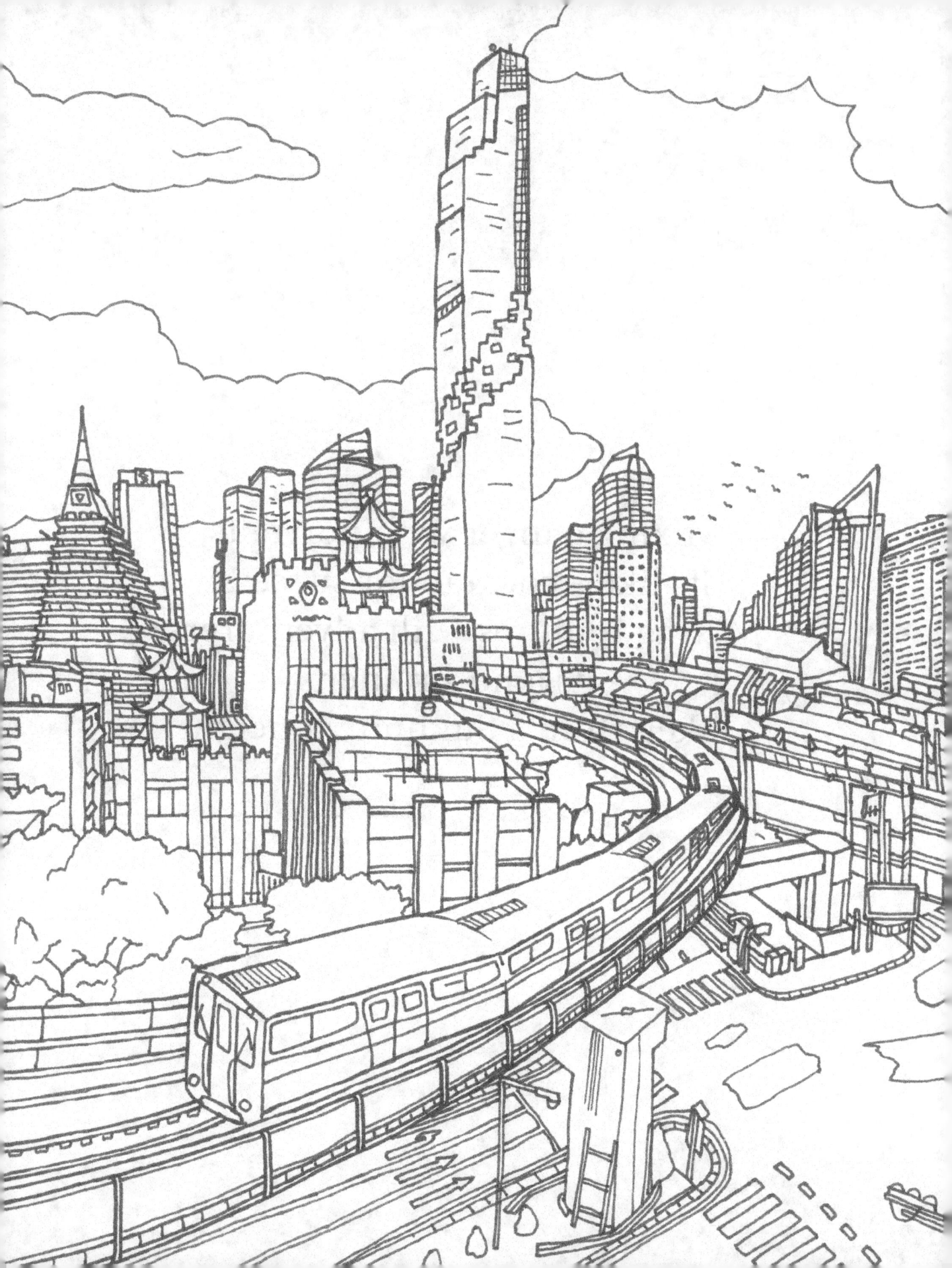

Mixing danger with portraits,
its like a cocktail for success.
Mixing rooftops with adventurers,
its a no-brainer.
Taken from a Sukhumvit height

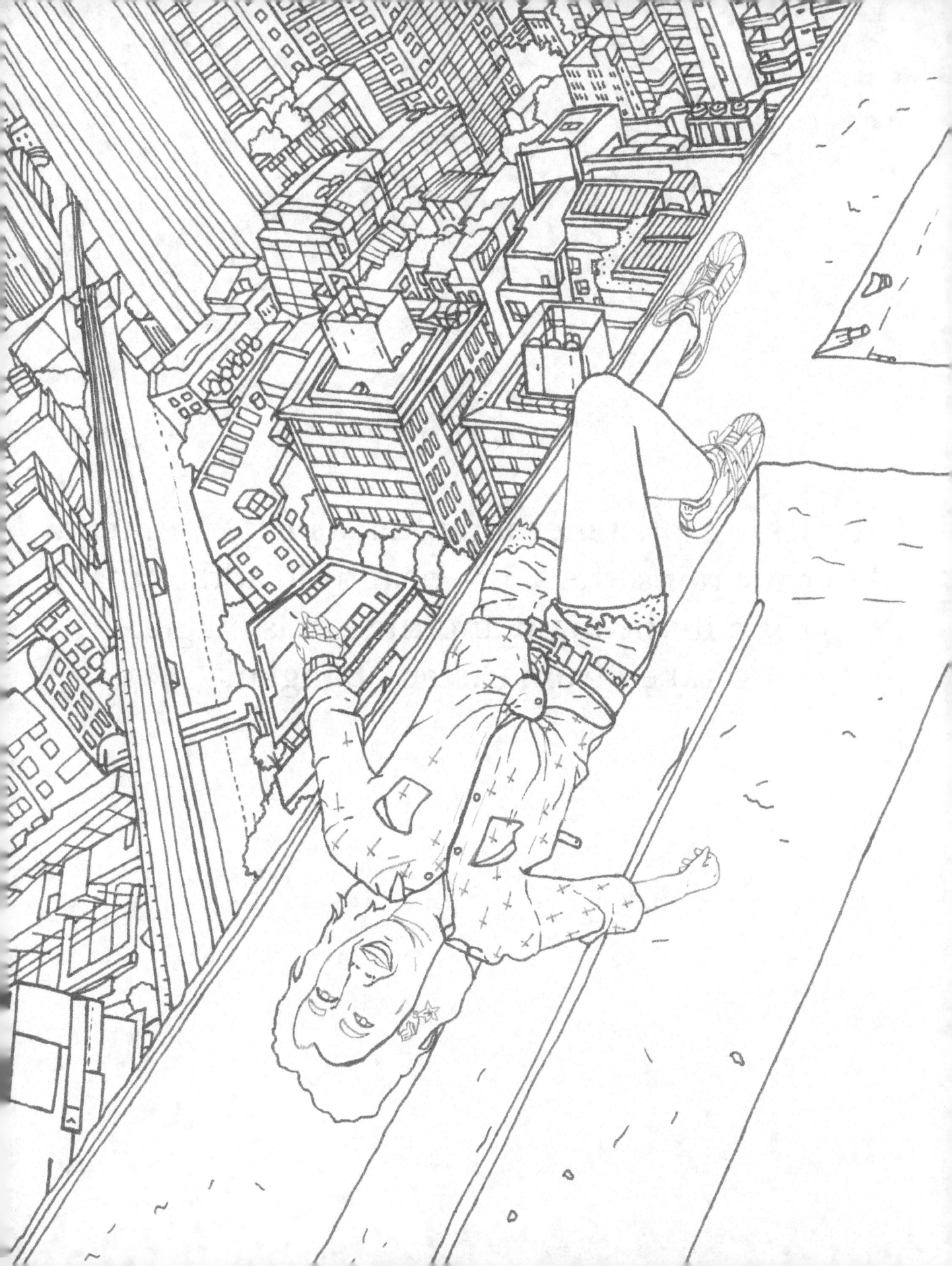

A parking lot, a motographer, a lucky moment. After the rains, the sky is beautiful, add to that a moon in the night and the sky is magical. Taken from eastern Bangkok

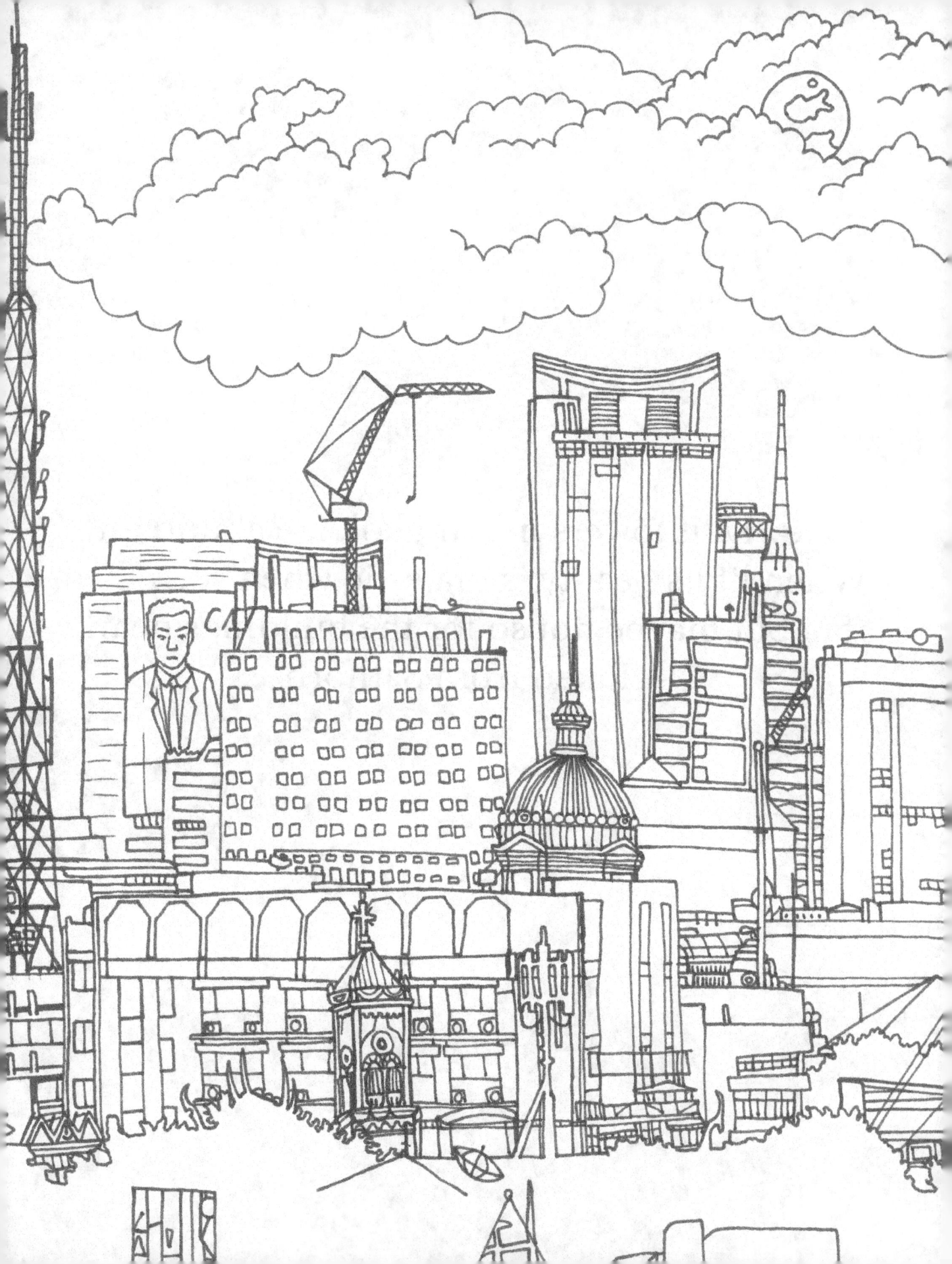

Newly lit towers in Bangkok are abundant. When lit its beauty is majestic when seen from afar, but maybe not so for the buildings nearby. Taken from Sathorn

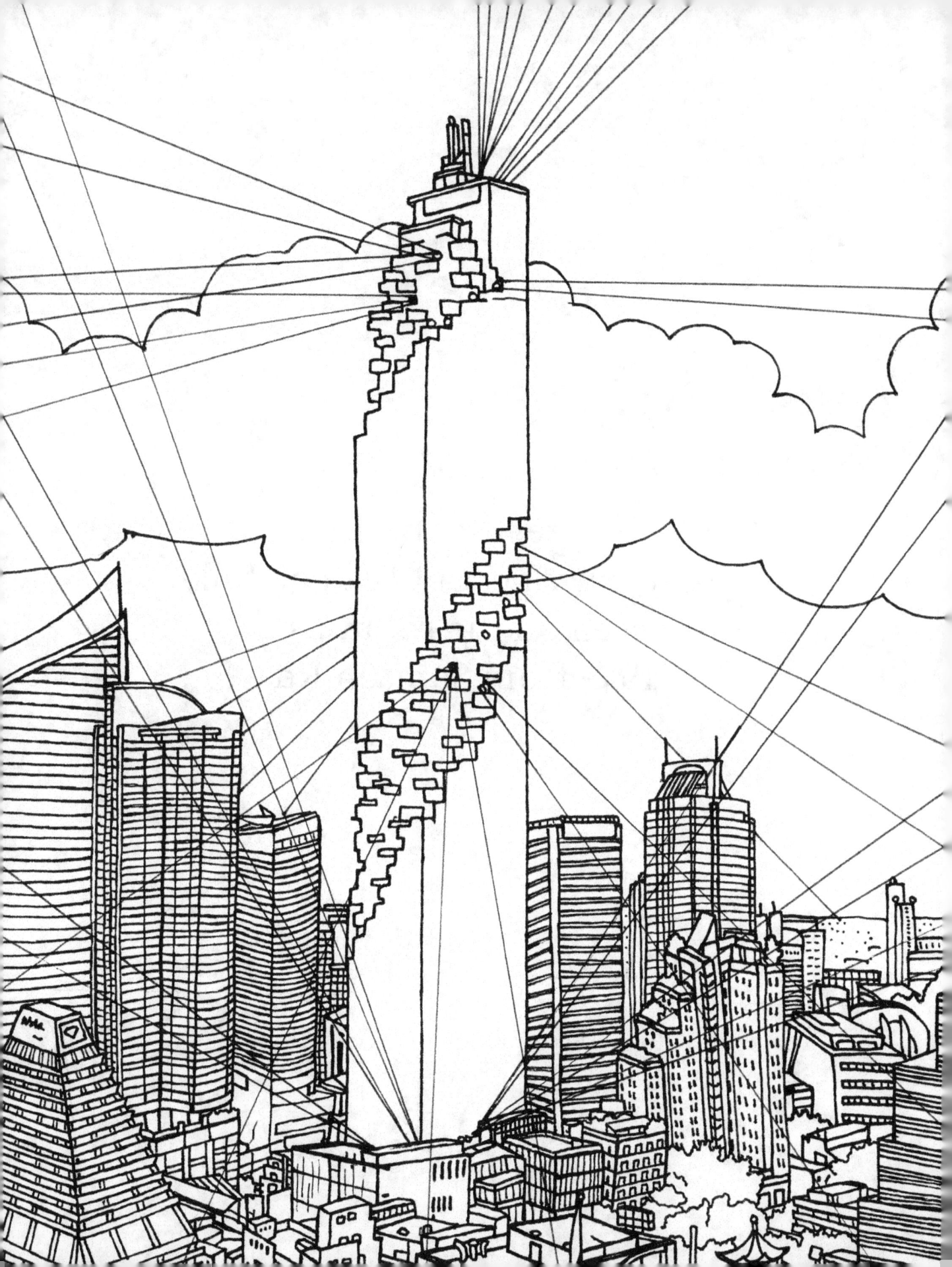

The Grand Palace, the traditional city with
a modern vibe, only can be fully
seen on the rooftops.
Take from Samsen Rd.

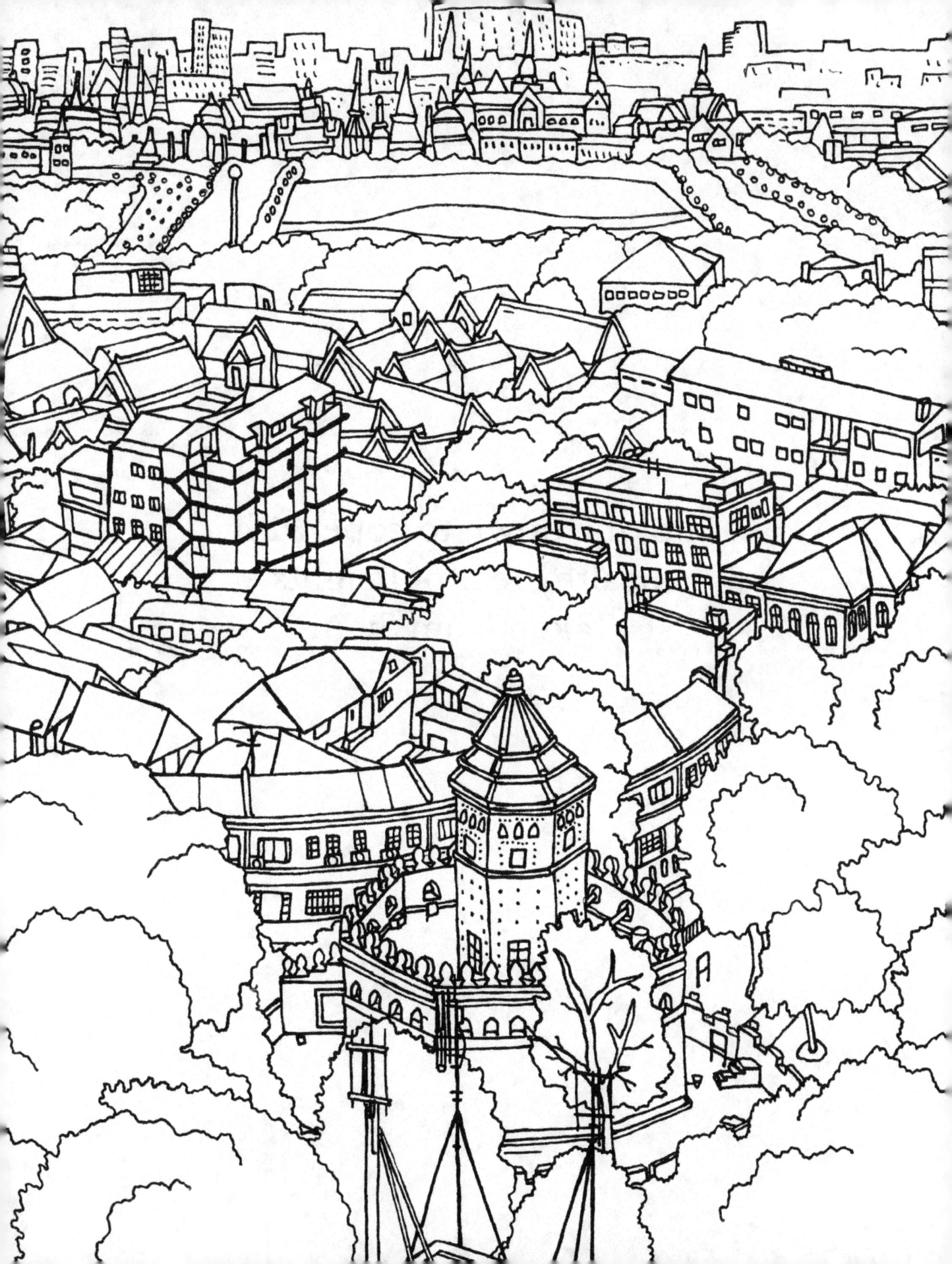

Looking down to cope with a
healthy fear of heights.
Taken from Siam

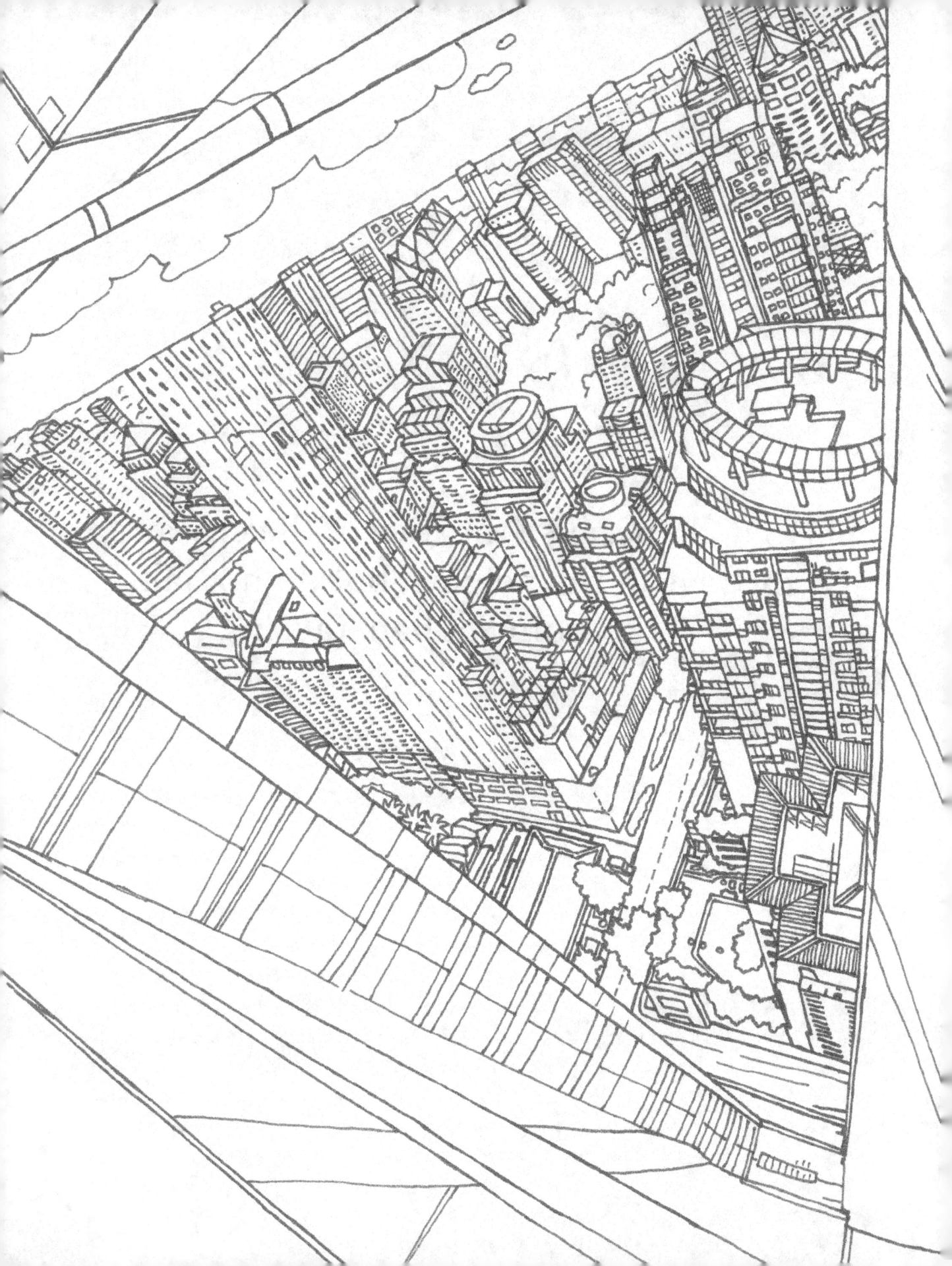

Do it all, because the love of the city and the love of the heights, but do not fall.
Take from Saphan Taksin

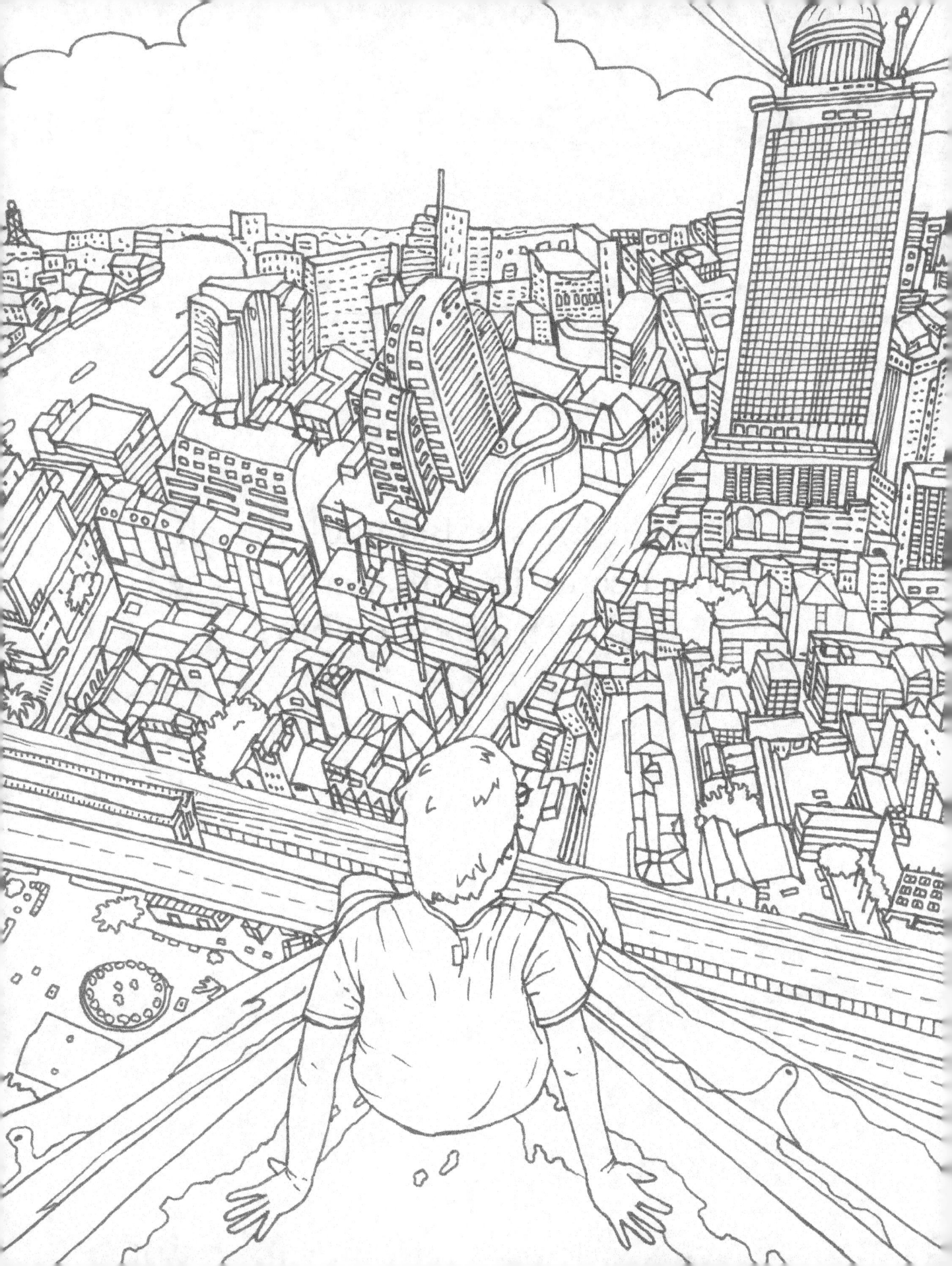

The outskirts of Bangkok has all
of the beauty in a smaller package.
Taken from Nontaburi

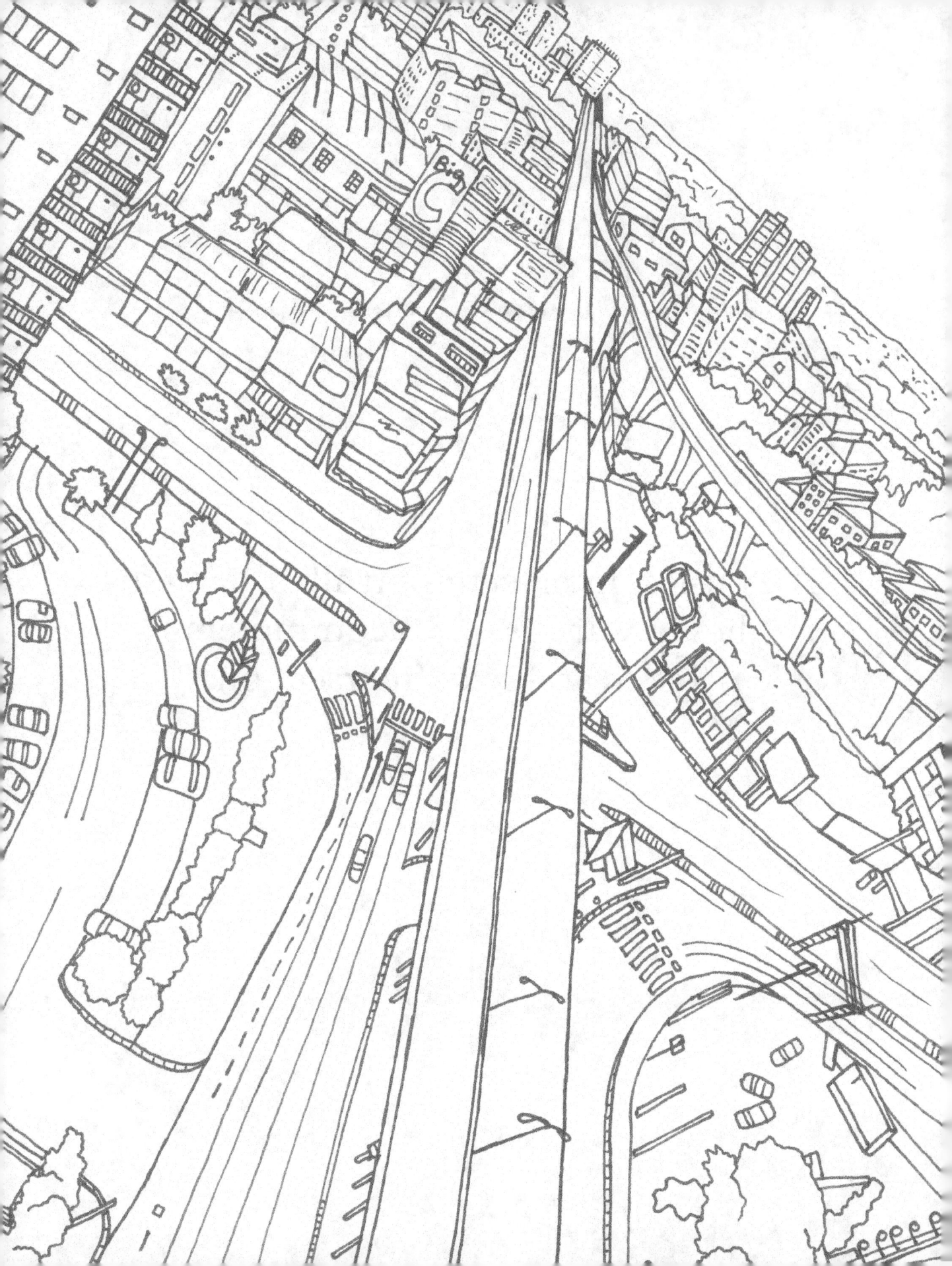

The busiest intersection in all of Bangkok
lies in wait, as do its commuters.
Taken at Asoke Intersection

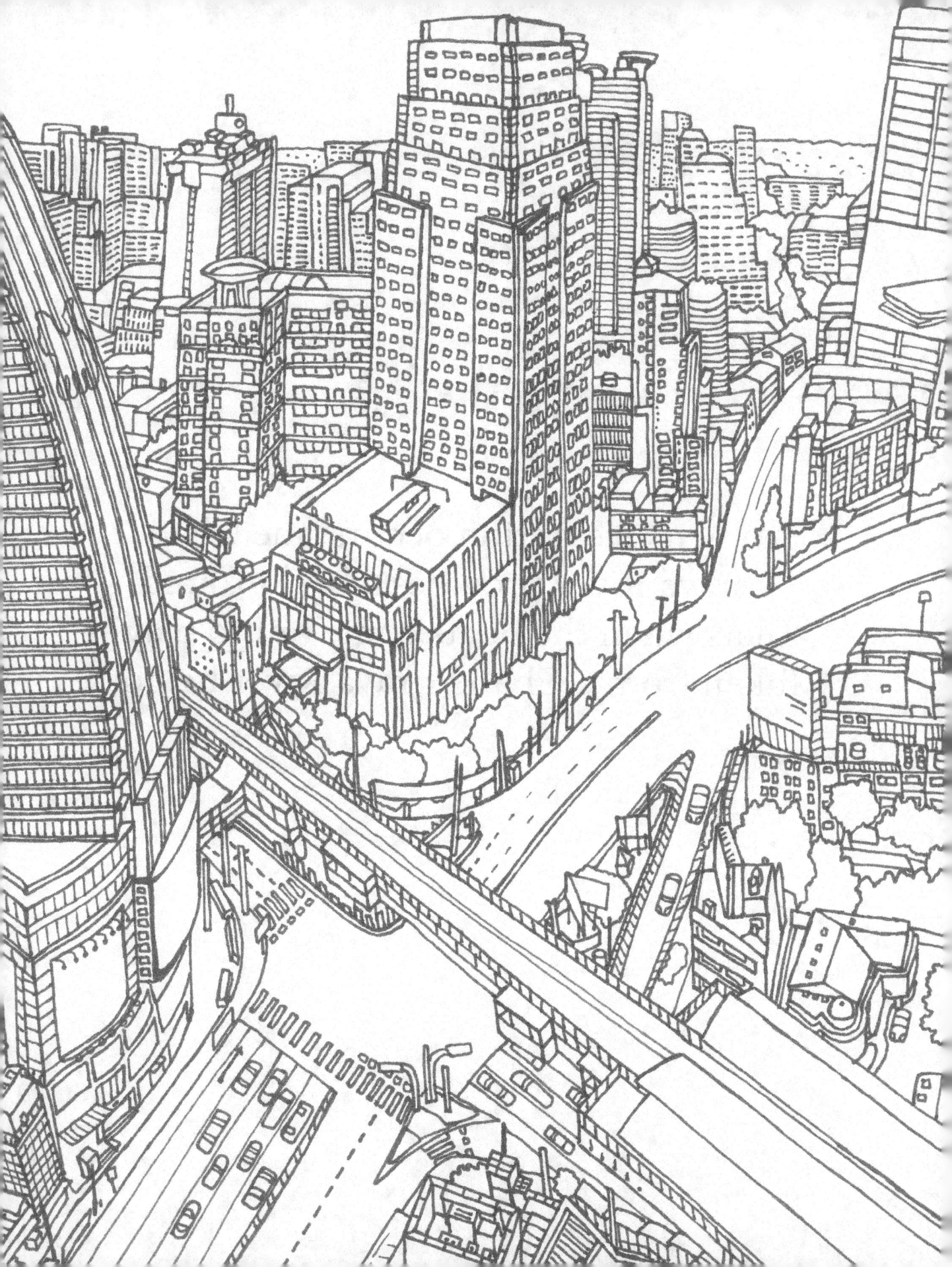

When celebration occurs, the Chao
Phraya River provides a background.
Thats when the boats come out to play.
Taken from a Chao Phraya River height

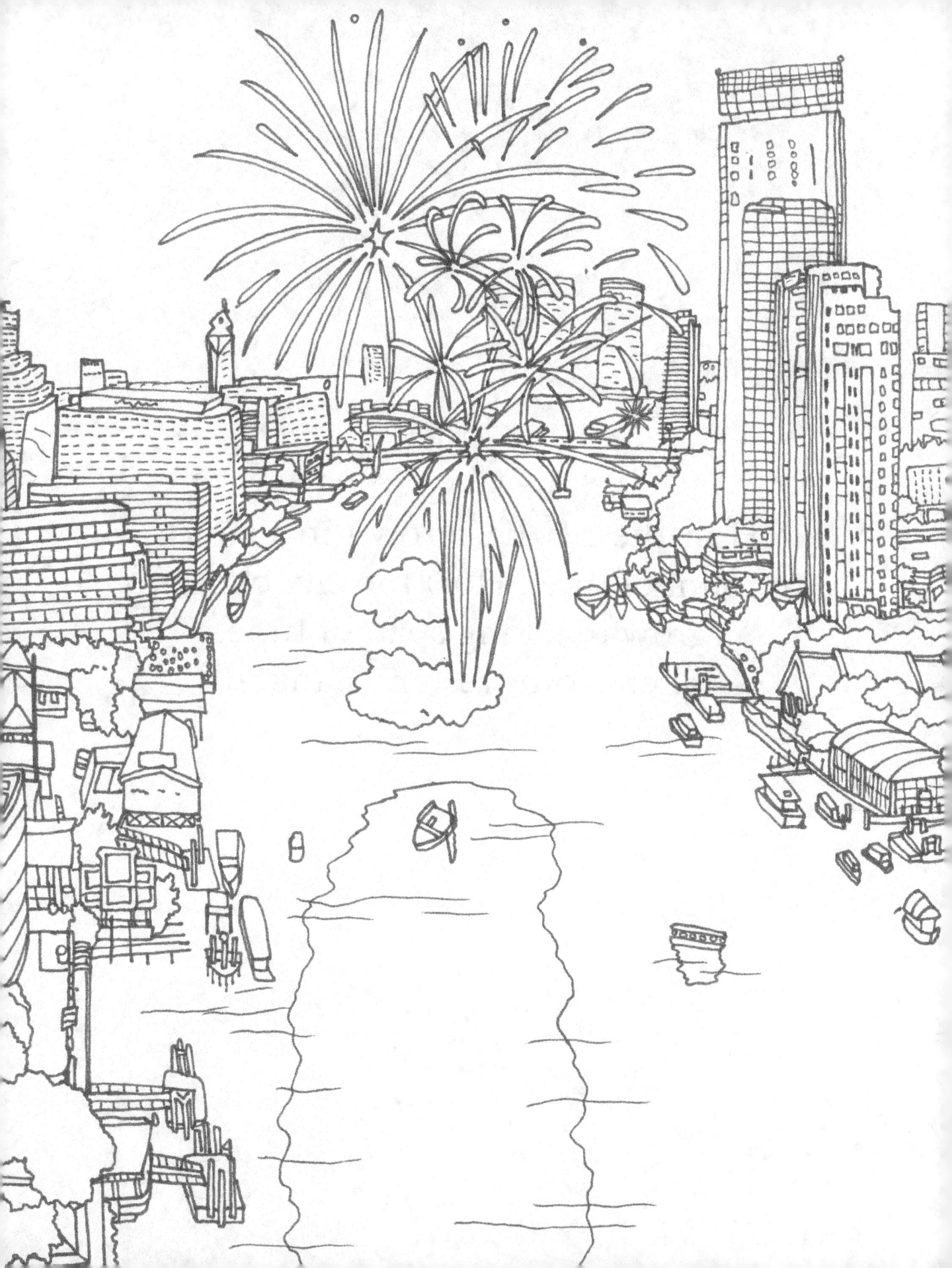

How the city has grown in a short amount of time. How the city chose to grow in a long span of time.
Taken from western Bangkok

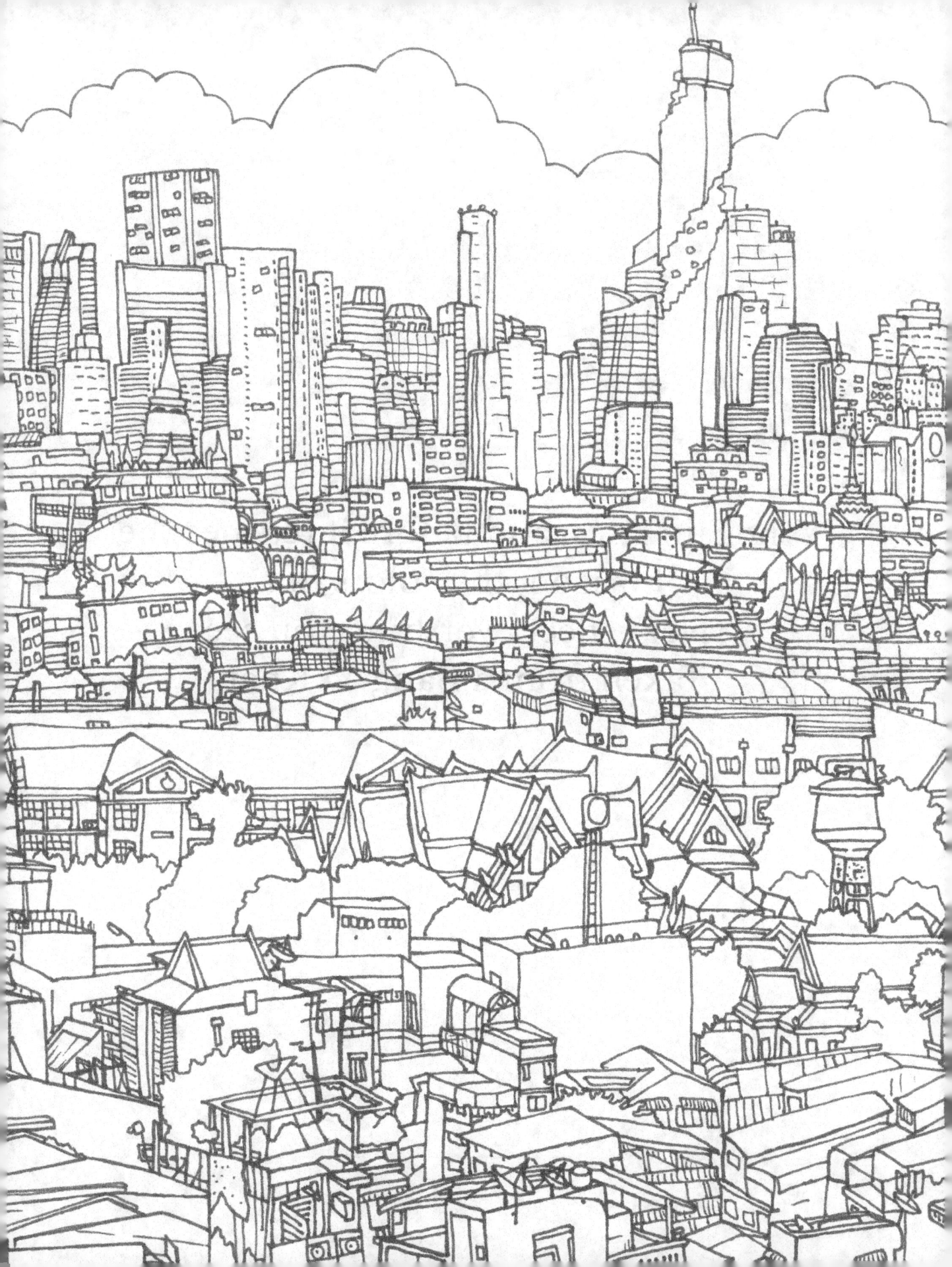

The Sun rises, and before it reaches the
horizon, the colors of a
river reflect everthing you see.
Taken from a Bang Yi Khan

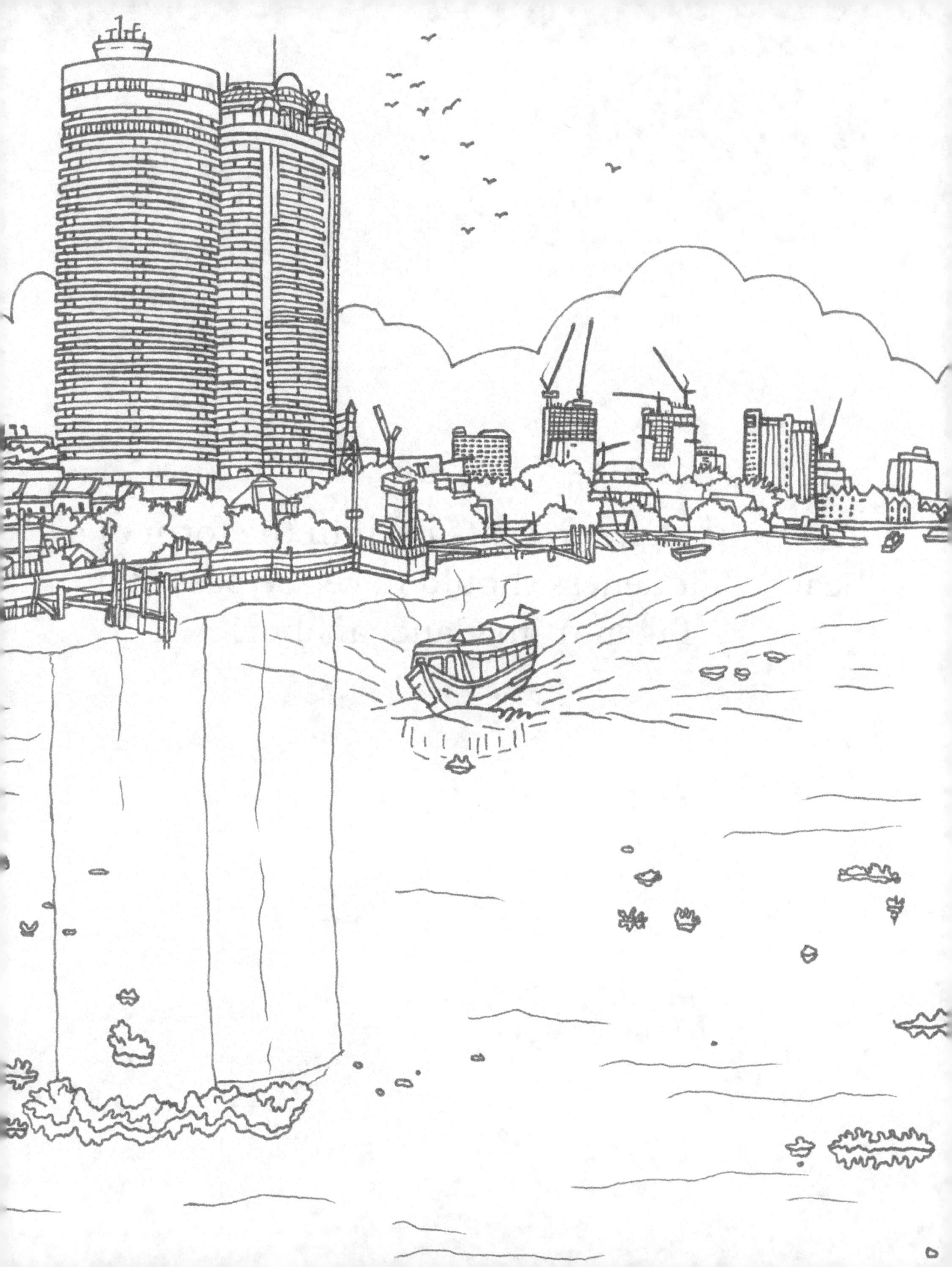

A unique sight presents itself in the form of a heart. Uniqueness should never be passed up. Taken from Ganchanaburi

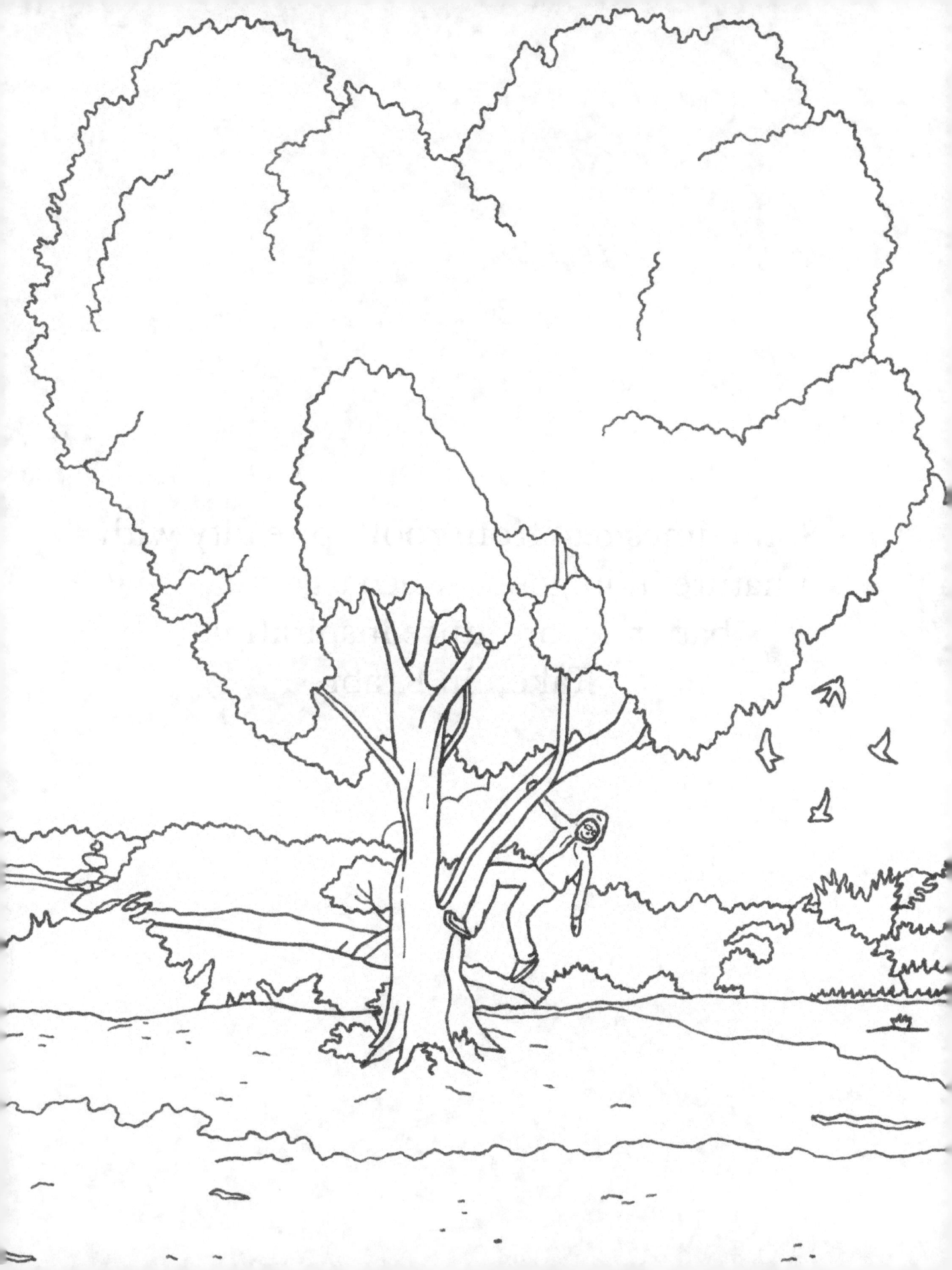

Sometimes rest from rooftop reality with a nature indulgence. Recharge the visual batteries for future inspiration.
Taken in Krabi

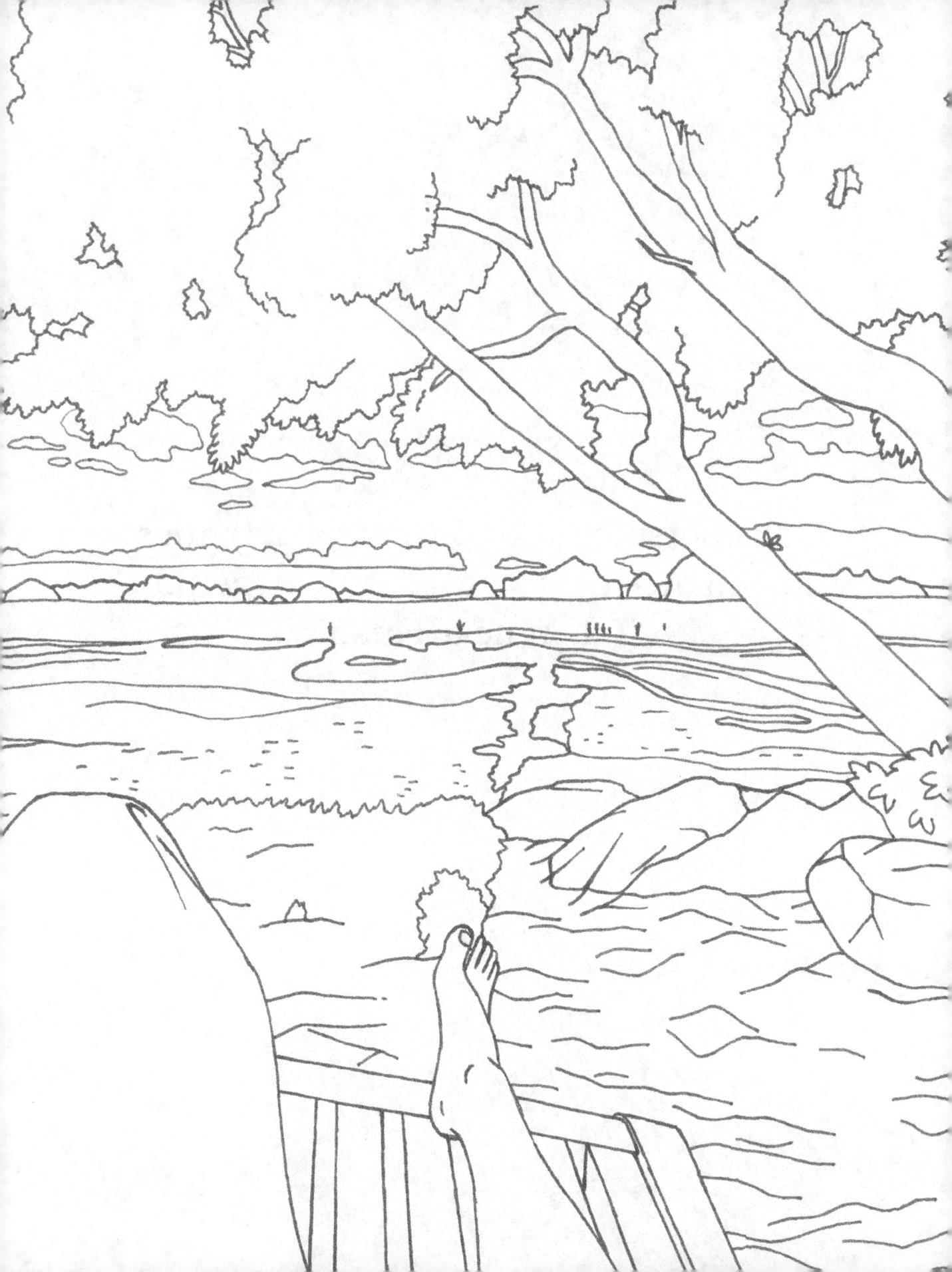

Immersion in Thai cultural activities
and enhance the photographic experiences.
Taken near Huahin

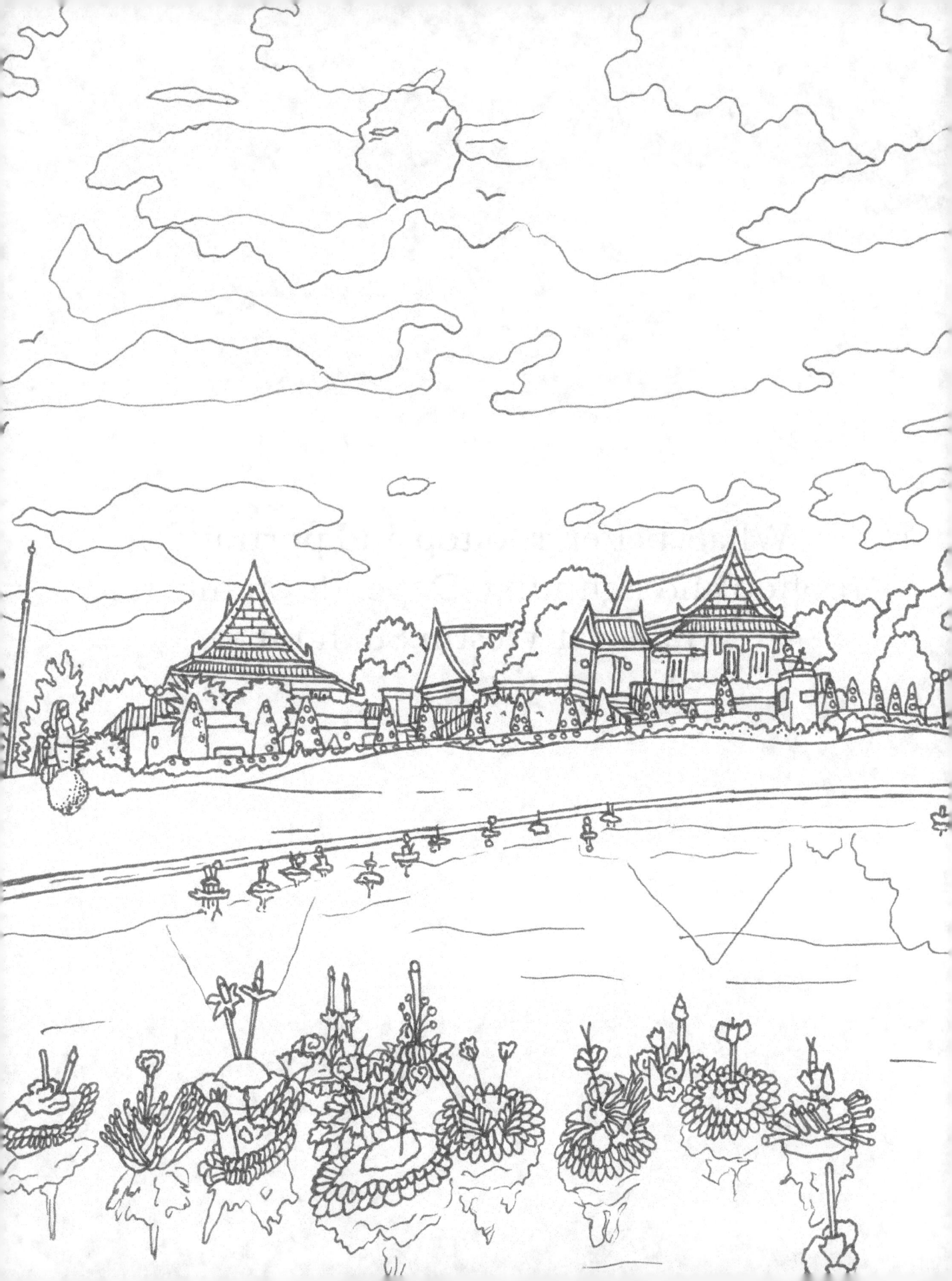

Whats better, rooftop and portraits or rooftop and lightning. Depends on the mood. Taken at Westin Sukhumvit

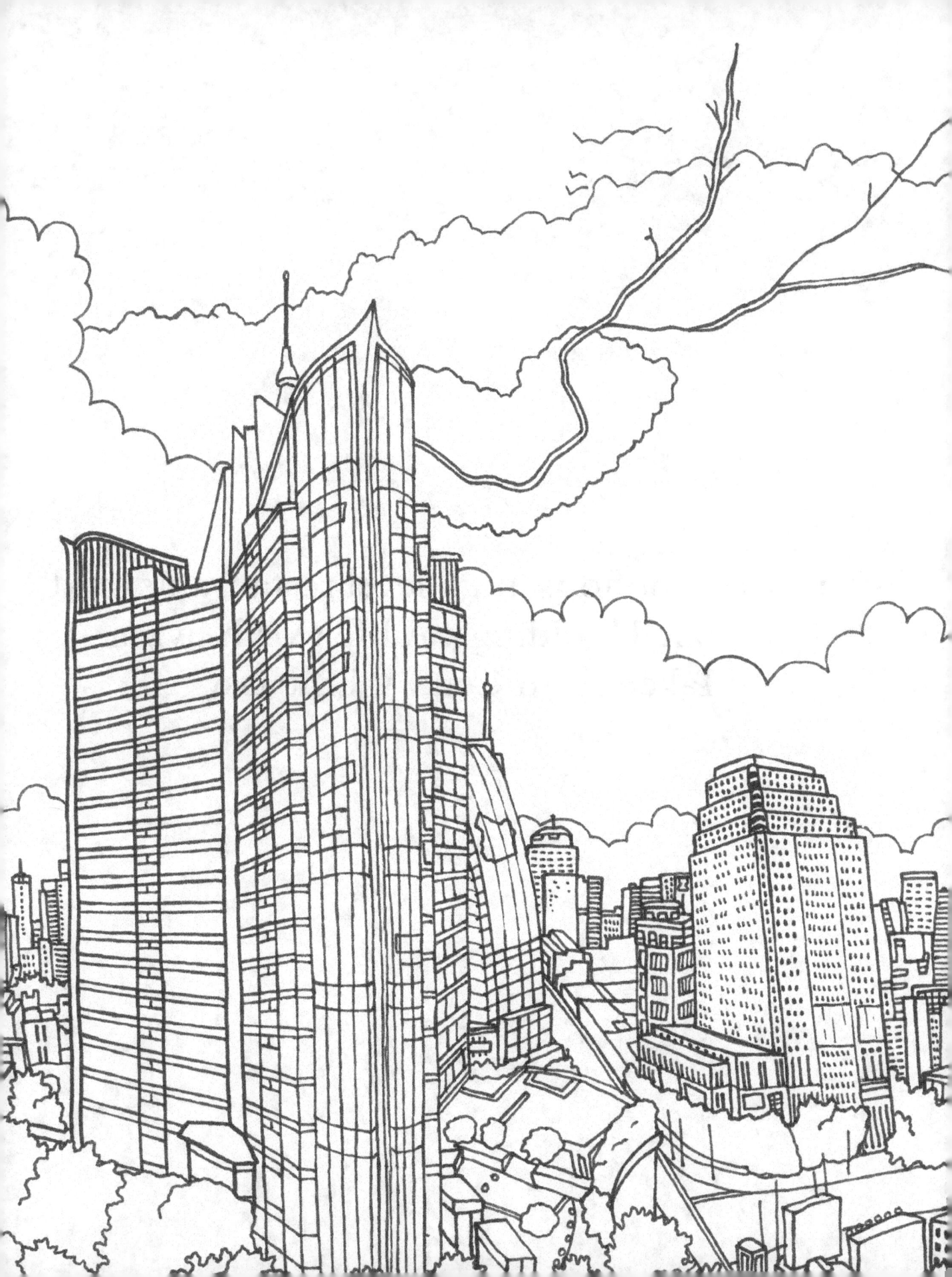

Bangkok's rooftops, high level restaurants, and abandoned buildings. A life worth living.
Taken from Central Embassy

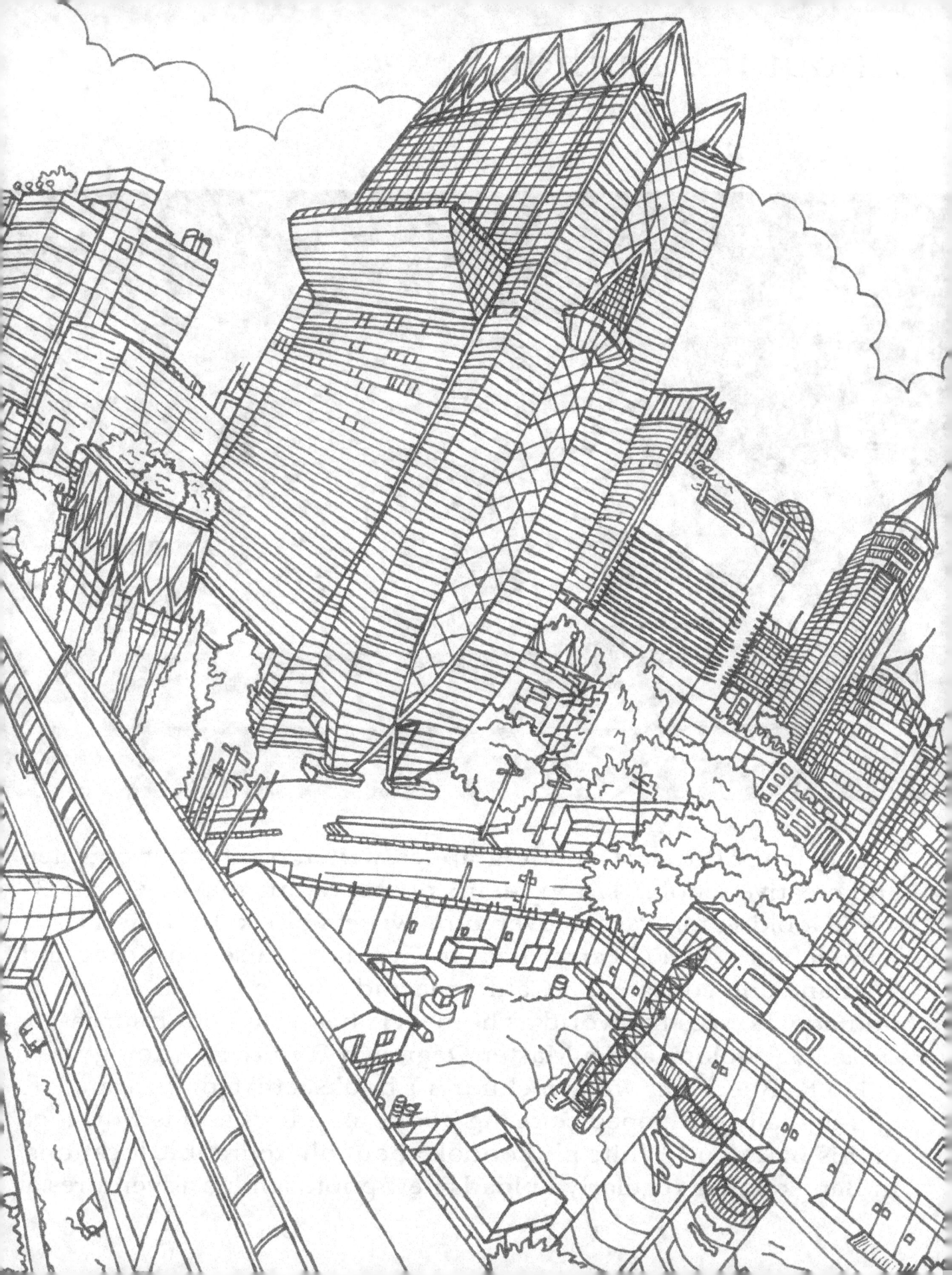

About the Author

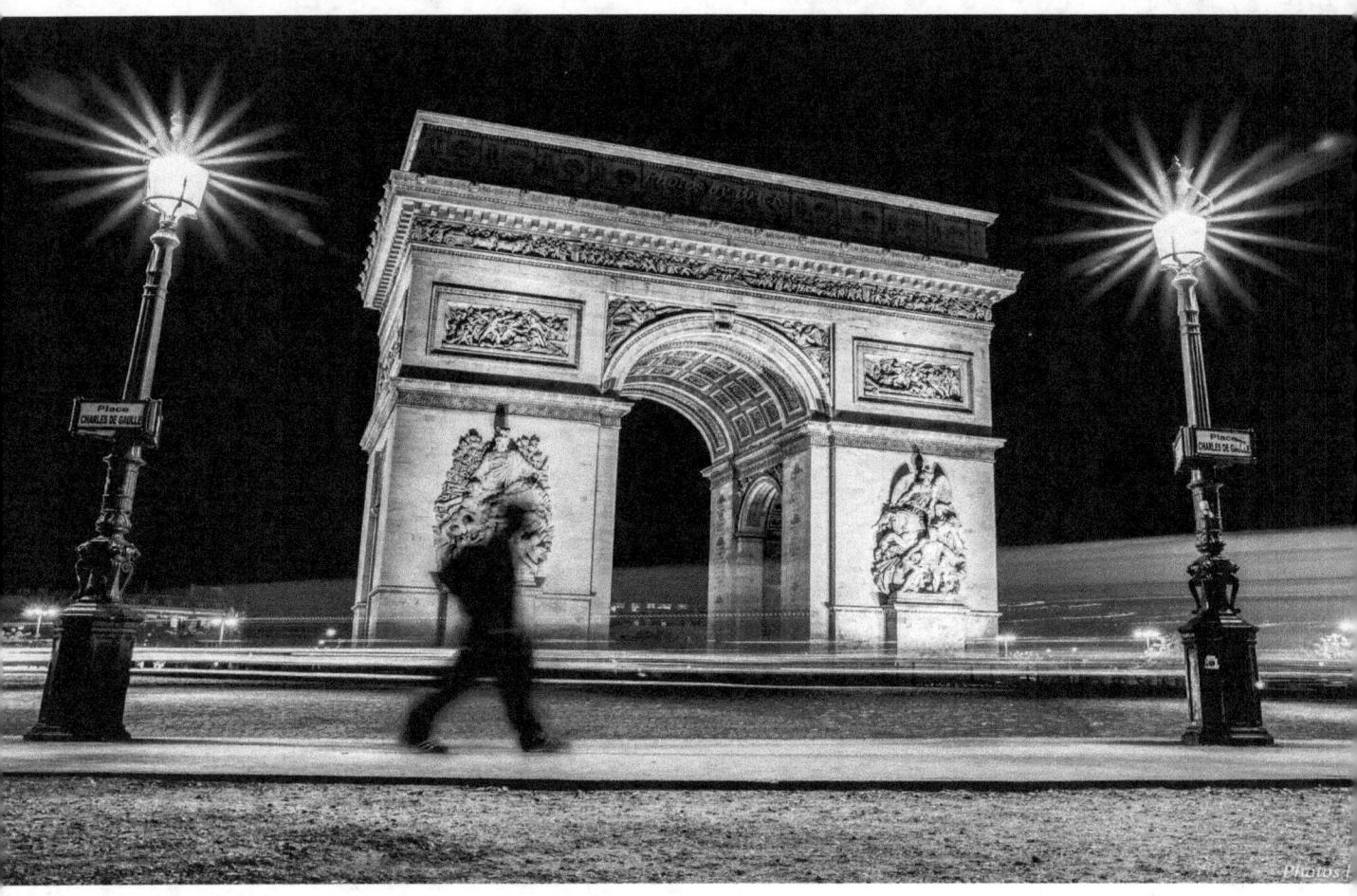

    Brian K Boeck is a photographer, writer, rooftopper, traveler and creative scholar. He began his photographic journey in 2013 while looking for ways to overcome writers block. Brian is a left hander, born on a US army base in Germany, raised in Korea and Thailand and educated in California and Chicago. He is a global nomad who sees the world as home. He has a Ph.D in International Psychology and a Master Degree in Family Psychology. Brian K. Boeck has written children's books, created illustrated and digitally developed coloring books for adults and is working on his Black and White photobook about photographic locations in Bangkok. He regularly uploads new photos of his adventures at